Mathscheck

Level 5

Paul Harling

Collins Educational

Published by Collins Educational
77– 85 Fulham Palace Road
London W6 8JB

An imprint of HarperCollins Publishers
© HarperCollins Publishers Ltd

First published 1993

ISBN 0 00 312584 X

Edited by: Joan Miller

Designed, produced and illustrated by: Gecko Ltd, Bicester, Oxon

Printed by: Martins the Printers, Berwick

Mathscheck

Mathscheck

Why use *Mathscheck*?

Mathscheck is a comprehensive set of photocopiable masters which can be used to monitor pupils' progress against the statutory Statements of Attainment of the National Curriculum for mathematics. The tests can be used as part of normal classwork and provide supportive documentation which can complement the continuous assessment of pupils made by the teacher.

Purposes of *Mathscheck*

Mathscheck enables teachers to:

1 Compare pupils' performance with the levels prescribed by the National Curriculum.

2 Identify pupils' achievements in relation to the National Curriculum levels so that teaching can be structured to meet their individual needs.

3 Group pupils in different ways for the teaching and learning of various aspects of the mathematics curriculum.

4 Gain an overall picture of pupils' progress so that they can devise long- and short-term teaching strategies.

5 Provide evidence of a pupil's achievements which can be used as a basis for discussion with the pupil, colleagues or parents or to ensure continuous teaching during transfer between classes and schools.

6 Decide more easily which levels of Standard Tasks are appropriate for a pupil.

Mathscheck and the National Curriculum

The National Curriculum

The National Curriculum sets out various stages in the growth of mathematical understanding, specifying ten levels of achievement across the five Attainment Targets.

Attainment Target 1: Using and applying mathematics

Attainment Target 2: Number

Attainment Target 3: Algebra

Attainment Target 4: Shape and space

Attainment Target 5: Handling data

Statements of Attainment

Pupils learn most effectively when they and the teacher are clear about what they have already experienced and understood and what they still have to learn. The Statements of Attainment provide basic objectives against which pupils' progress can be monitored. Systematic assessment of the Statements of Attainment provides an important sense of progress for both teacher and pupil.

This does not mean that teaching should concentrate only on the Statements of Attainment or that pupils should be taught in a strict level-by-level sequence. The Programme of Study that forms the core of the National Curriculum and provides breadth and depth of learning includes elements that are more appropriately assessed as part of the everyday interaction of teacher and pupil.

Types of Statement of Attainment

There are three main types of Statement of Attainment, explained in the National Curriculum Council Document 'Mathematics: Non-Statutory Guidance (1991)'.

1 **General Statements of Attainment which combine several elements of the associated Programme of Study.**

2 **Statements of Attainment which represent a single key idea within a group of elements in the Programme of Study.**

3 **Statements of Attainment which isolate a very important element of the Programme of Study.**

There are also elements of the Programme of Study at some levels which, for the purposes of assessment, are related to part of a Statement of Attainment at a subsequent level. Where this occurs, the test notes provide clarification.

The *Mathscheck* materials

Levels

The tests are arranged in accordance with the statutory levels of the National Curriculum. Each of the nine books contains tests for a single level of the National Curriculum, apart from the first book which includes tests for both level 1 and level 2.

Criterion referencing

The tests are criterion referenced and therefore assess each pupil's level of performance against a benchmark of specific mathematical content and the associated skills.

Attainment Target 1

Attainment Target 1 is different from the other four Attainment Targets. Whereas Attainment Targets 2–5 describe the stages of progression in knowledge, skills and understanding, Attainment Target 1 is concerned with using and applying that knowledge, skill and understanding. The Non-Statutory Guidance to the National Curriculum (1989) points out that:

> …work related to Attainment Target 1…cannot be tackled in isolation from the rest of the Programmes of Study….. Using and applying mathematics…should stretch across and permeate all other work in mathematics, providing both the means to, and the rationale for, the progressive development of knowledge, skills and understanding in mathematics.
> (Page D2, paragraph 1.5.)

The wide ranging purpose of Attainment Target 1 means that specific pencil-and-paper tests are inappropriate. Such tests would assess performance only in relation to a chosen task. What is needed is a broader overview of the pupil's performance across the whole range of mathematical work.

Therefore *Mathscheck* contains a carefully researched checklist of 'behaviours' of pupils who are working effectively at each level. This should complement the teacher's own assessment of the pupils' ability and understanding.

If a pupil is achieving most of the specified items at a given level while working mathematically on the content or skills detailed in related levels of several of the Attainment Targets 2–5, then that pupil will be working successfully at that level of Attainment Target 1.

To clarify the sense of progression in Attainment Target 1, checklists for three consecutive related levels are included in each book:

Tests (for Ma2–5)	Checklists (for Ma1)
Levels 1 and 2	Levels 1, 2 and 3
Level 3	Levels 2, 3 and 4
Level 4	Levels 3, 4 and 5
Level 6	Levels 5, 6 and 7
Level 7	Levels 6, 7 and 8
Level 8	Levels 7, 8 and 9
Level 9	Levels 8, 9 and 10
Level 10	Levels 8, 9 and 10

The checklists allow for the recording of observed success across the full range of Attainment Targets 2–5.

Organisation of the material

The tests are arranged in the same order as the Statements of Attainment in the National Curriculum. Each test is clearly labelled in the top left-hand corner to show to which Attainment Target and Statement of Attainment it refers (e.g. Ma 4/5d).

For most Statements of Attainment the appropriate test items have been included on one or two pages. However, other Statements of Attainment are more extensive and, for these, additional pages are provided. Each sheet states whether it is 'One sheet only', 'First of two sheets', etc.

Parallel forms

For each Statement of Attainment, two parallel forms of the test (marked Series I and Series II at the top of the sheets) have been included in each book. This means the teacher can re-test if appropriate, or that pairs of pupils can sit together and work on parallel, but independent, assessments of any Statement of Attainment.

Using *Mathscheck*

When to use Mathscheck

Mathscheck has been designed to be part of a teacher's continuous assessment of pupil attainment and progress. Therefore the tests should be used on an ad hoc basis, not in a block at the end of a term or year.

After pupils have been working within an area of the mathematics curriculum, *Mathscheck* can be used to provide a corresponding pencil-and-paper assessment, directly linked with the appropriate Statement of Attainment.

Evidence

The tests provide evidence of achievement on a continuous basis. Each of the sheets has space for the pupil's name and the date, so that the sequence of achievement can be seen. The date on which each test is completed and the Statements of Attainment achieved can also be noted on the simple record sheets supplied.

Preparation by the teacher

Space for working is provided on the sheets and for the vast majority of the tests little or no preparation is required. However, in a few cases, the teacher will need to organise a simple practical situation, provide simple equipment and paper, or ensure the availability of a microcomputer with suitable software to fulfil the requirements of the National Curriculum.

Time limits

There are no time limits assigned to the tests. Pupils should be given the time they need in order to demonstrate their knowledge and skill.

Marking

The tests need a minimum amount of marking and facsimile pages containing the answers are provided at the back of the book.

Oral presentation

Some of the tests, particularly at the earlier levels can be presented orally. This is useful for second-language learners. Where the National Curriculum requires pupils to read the instructions for themselves, the notes for particular levels make this clear. General reading requirements have been kept to a minimum wherever possible so that mathematics alone can be the major focus of the assessment.

Special educational needs

The tests are related to levels rather than to ages or year groups and can be cut and pasted in any form. This means they can be used with slower pupils who might be overwhelmed by a full page of activities. The mathematical progress of these pupils can then be frequently assessed, at their own pace, without causing them undue stress.

Shy, withdrawn or difficult pupils

The tests in *Mathscheck* are particularly useful for assessing the progress of shy, withdrawn or difficult pupils who do not easily relate to other children. Because the tests are individual, informal and short, they can be used as part of normal classwork.

What constitutes 'attainment'?

Strictly speaking pupils can be said to have mastered a particular Statement of Attainment when they achieve total success in all relevant work they do. However, some mistakes are inevitable. The decision as to whether a Statement of Attainment has been attained depends almost totally on the professional judgement of the teacher, especially as not all aspects of the Statements of Attainment can be tested with a paper and pencil. As a rough guide, pupils should give correct answers in approximately 75 per cent of the tasks if they are to be credited with attainment. The reasons for errors are more important than the number of errors. In many cases the method used is a more important indicator of achievement than the answer.

Following up pupils' mistakes

Pupils should be encouraged to discuss what has been achieved on a test, to confirm progress or to highlight aspects which need more experience or practice. Mistakes can occur for various reasons and each requires a different response from the teacher.

1 Carelessness

Everyone makes careless mistakes from time to time but these can be minimised by encouraging the pupils to see assessment as an important and beneficial part of learning, on which they need to concentrate fully. Pupils should be encouraged to read the tasks carefully and to ask for clarification if in doubt about what they are being asked to do.

2 Momentary distraction or failed memory

A good deal of mathematics requires pupils to absorb and memorise facts. Sometimes, pupils fail because they have insufficient experience on which to build the act of remembering. Practice is often the key to success. It is worth noting that some pupils are able to respond correctly to a verbal question but may be confused by the written word. Often a small hint may be enough to remind them of something they actually know.

3 Lack of basic experience of the concept, skill or process

If a pupil's responses continue to show a lack of awareness of the concept, skill or process, this should be taken as a clear indication that this area needs to be revisited by the pupil.

4 Lack of experience of the style of the question or task

Given the vast range of types and styles of tasks found in the many published schemes, a pupil may simply be unfamiliar with what to do to answer a question. In this case, rewording the question or task will usually help and need not affect the validity of the overall assessment of the Statement of Attainment.

5 Lack of understanding

Although the teacher may be sure that the pupil has experienced the concept, skill or process, discussion may show that the pupil has simply not understood the work. In this case, the teacher should provide further experience, starting at the point at which the pupil begins to show lack of understanding. This might mean a return to practical first principles, or a refinement of the vocabulary associated with the topic.

6 Choice of an inappropriate or incorrect procedure

Excessive concentration on a single way of calculating, for example, may confuse a pupil. Practice in 'reading' mathematics and interpreting different forms of question is essential at all stages of pupil development.

Notes for Level 5

Please read this page before using the assessment sheets

Ma 2/5a
(pages 12-13 and 39-40)

Pupils should **not** use a calculator.
Tasks 9 and 10 require pupils to work mentally. No working should be seen for attainment to be agreed.

Ma 2/5b
(pages 14-15 and 41-42)

A calculator can be used. The elements of the PoS concerned with unitary ratios and the notion of scale are assessed as part of Ma 2/6a and Ma 4/6b.

Ma 2/5c
(pages 16 and 43)

Use of a calculator is recommended, but is not essential.

Ma 2/5d
(pages 17-18 and 44-45)

This SoA is essentially practical and further assessment of the knowledge, concepts and skills should be undertaken in context. The assessment paper concentrates on the numerical aspects and a calculator can be used when appropriate.
The element of the PoS concerned with index notation is assessed as part of Ma 2/8a.

Ma 3/5b
(pages 21-22 and 48-49)

The element of the PoS concerned with coordinates is assessed as part of Ma 3/6c.

Ma 4/5a
(pages 23-25 and 50-52)

Because the construction of 3-D models relies largely on accurate drawing and measurement of angles the skills involved form the bulk of the assessment. The third sheet requires pupils to construct simple 3-D models. If a pupil has difficulty recognising a drawing of a 3-D shape, make available solid examples and materials, or offer further explanation.

Ma 4/5b
(pages 26-28 and 53-55)

Some of the standard terminology used in the assessment may be subject to slight variation depending upon the published scheme used by the pupil. Protractors should **not** be available. The angles are to be calculated from the given information.

Ma 4/5c
(pages 29 and 56)

The element of the PoS concerned with coordinates is assessed as part of Ma 3/6c. If a pupil has difficulty recognising a drawing of a 3-D shape please make solid examples and materials available, or offer further explanation.

Ma 4/5d
(pages 30-31 and 57-58)

The element of the PoS concerned with measurement of a circle is assessed as part of Ma 4/6d and Ma 4/7d. If a pupil has difficulty recognising a drawing of a 3-D shape please make solid examples and materials available, or offer further explanation.

Ma 5/5a
(pages 32 and 59)

A computer database **must** be available to provide evidence of attainment. A pupil's work should be checked after each activity. Further checking of the skills would be desirable, perhaps using the database files supplied with most educational database packages.

Ma 5/5b and Ma 5/5c
(pages 33-36 and 60-63)

The skills involved in these Statements of Attainment are best assessed in the context of general work on handling data in a variety of cross-curricular contexts. The activities on the assessment sheets are frameworks for the spot-checking skills, and can be adapted to other contexts if felt to be appropriate.

Name _____ *Date of birth* _____

National Curriculum Level Record

Write the date of attainment of each SoA and comment as appropriate

	Statement of Attainment	Date	Comments
Ma1 Using and applying maths	a Carry through a task by breaking it down into smaller, more manageable forms		
	b Interpret information presented in a variety of mathematical forms		
	c Make a generalisation and test it		
Ma2 Numbers	a Use an appropriate non-calculator method to multiply or divide two numbers		
	b Find fractions or percentages of quantities		
	c Refine estimation by 'trial and improvement' methods		
	d Use units in context		
Ma3 Algebra	a Follow instructions to generate sequences		
	b Express a simple function symbolically		
Ma4 Shape and Space	a Use accurate measurement and drawing in constructing 3-D models		
	b Use properties of shape to justify explanations		
	c Use networks to solve problems		
	d Find areas of plane shapes or volumes of simple solids		
Ma5 Handling Data	a Use a computer database to draw conclusions		
	b Design and use an observation sheet to collect data		
	c Interpret statistical diagrams		
	d Use an appropriate method for estimating probabilities		

Mathscheck
KS1/KS2

Name _____ **Date of birth** _____

National Curriculum Summative Record

Ring the SoAs when attained

Level	Using and applying mathematics 1	Number 2	Algebra 3	Shape and space 4	Handling data 5	Comments
1	a b c	a b	a	a b c	a	
2	a b c	a b c d	a b	a b	a b	
3	a b c d	a b c d e	a b	a b c	a b c	
4	a b c d	a b c d e	a b c	a b c d	a b c d	
5	a b c	a b c d	a b	a b c d	a b c d	
6	a b c	a b	a b c	a b c d	a b c d	

KEY STAGE 1 (Levels 1–3)
KEY STAGE 2 (Levels 4–6)

Name _____ **Date of birth** _____

National Curriculum Summative Record

Ring the SoAs when attained

	ATs / Level	Using and applying mathematics 1	Number 2	Algebra 3	Shape and space 4	Handling data 5	Comments
KEY STAGE 3	**3**	a b c d	a b c d e	a b	a b c	a b c	
	4	a b c d	a b c d e	a b c	a b c d	a b c d	
	5	a b c	a b c d	a b	a b c d	a b c d	
	6	a b c	a b	a b c	a b c d	a b c d	
KEY STAGE 4	**7**	a b	a b c	a b	a b c d	a b c	
	8	a b	a b c	a b c	a b c	a b c	
	9	a b	a b	a b c	a b c	a b c	
	10	a b	a	a b c d	a	a b c	

(a) Pupils should be able to identify and obtain information necessary to solve problems. *Can the pupil:*	Tick when attainment has been observed when working in:			
	Ma2	**Ma3**	**Ma4**	**Ma5**
i Recall and use a range of materials employed in previous activities?				
ii Recall and use a range of methods employed in previous activities?				
iii Personally plan a sequence of activities to carry out a task?				
iv Take an active part in cooperative group planning of a task?				
v Use a clearly articulated approach to a task?				
vi Choose and use materials and resources directly appropriate to a task?				
vii Attempt to give support to another group member when asked?				
viii Discuss a range of methods with other group members and the teacher?				
(b) Pupils should be able to interpret situations mathematically, using appropriate symbols and diagrams. *Can the pupil:*				
i Refine the data of a real-world situation into a numerical or geometric form to facilitate calculation or observation of patterns?				
ii Record work done in:				
a pictorial form				
a written form				
a diagrammatic form				
a graphical form				
symbolic form?				
iii Recognise the need for clear and systematic recording to aid understanding and interpretation?				
iv Use various forms of recording as evidence to substantiate verbal explanations?				
(c) Pupils should be able to give some justification for their solutions to problems. *Can the pupil:*				
i Suggest/predict possible solutions to problems?				
ii Recognise and find patterns of numbers, shapes and symbols?				
iii Suggest clear explanations or 'definitions' of mathematical patterns?				
iv Find appropriate examples which confirm or invalidate predictions?				
(d) Pupils should be able to make generalisations. *Can the pupil:*				
i Recognise and describe relationships between items of information?				
ii Suggest other possible contexts in which similar solutions might be observed?				
iii Flexibly follow alternative lines of thought?				
iv Recognise when an investigation has reached a 'dead end'?				
v Change to an alternative line of thought without being asked to do so?				

Name _____ Date of birth _____

Using and applying mathematics

		Ma2	Ma3	Ma4	Ma5
(a) Pupils should be able to carry through a task by breaking it down into smaller, more manageable tasks. *Tick when attainment has been observed when working in:*					
Can the pupil:					
i	Personally plan an effective sequence of activities to carry out a task?				
ii	Choose and use a wide range of appropriate mathematical concepts, skills and processes to tackle a task?				
iii	Discuss which actions and processes are appropriate (or inappropriate) for a task?				
iv	Decide whether available information is relevant or irrelevant to the task?				
v	Modify a chosen approach as unforeseen lines of thought emerge?				
vi	Review progress with guidance from the teacher?				
vii	Work effectively as an active, participating member of groups of various sizes?				
viii	Work individually on an extended personal topic in mathematics?				
(b) Pupils should be able to interpret information presented in a variety of mathematical forms.					
Can the pupil:					
i	Explain and/or discuss own presentations of information in oral, written or diagrammatic or constructed forms?				
ii	Understand and interpret other pupils' presentations of information?				
iii	Make sense of media representations of facts, ideas or processes?				
iv	Recognise misleading presentations of information?				
v	Suggest appropriate ways to improve the clarity of everyday presentations of information?				
vi	Operate competently at a personal level in the real world of timetables, schedules and the like?				
(c) Pupils should be able to make a generalisation and test it.					
Can the pupil:					
i	Systematically follow verbal, written or diagrammatic instructions?				
ii	Organise information from the environment in a 'mathematical' way?				
iii	Recognise and discuss clues to possible patterns in findings?				
iv	Use techniques such as 'exhaustive listing' to organise numerical data or information?				
v	Make 'mathematical' statements to identify the rules or generalisations evident in patterns?				
vi	Test the validity of statements by using examples from within the information itself?				

Name _____ **Date of birth** _____

Using and applying mathematics

		Ma2	Ma3	Ma4	Ma5
(a) Pupils should be able to pose their own questions or design a task in a given context.	*Tick when attainment has been observed when working in:*				
Can the pupil:					
i	Show sound understanding of relevant concepts at appropriate levels in ATs 2 to 5?				
ii	Make sense of the quantity and quality of given information?				
iii	List the problems needing solution in a task?				
iv	Design and carry out a task with minimal reference to the teacher?				
v	Seek out missing information?				
vi	Choose and use appropriate resources independently and with clear purpose?				
vii	Use 'trial and improvement' methods with confidence?				
viii	Independently extend a given task to examine linked contexts?				
(b) Pupils should be able to examine critically the mathematical presentation of information.					
Can the pupil:					
i	Confidently use any of the oral, written, pictorial or diagrammatic modes of recording for different purposes?				
ii	Combine two or more different modes of recording?				
iii	Support the findings shown by one mode of recording by use of a complementary mode?				
iv	Interpret a variety of school-based, and media-derived presentations of information?				
v	Effectively describe and discuss the strengths and weaknesses of a variety of presentations of information?				
(c) Pupils should be able to make a generalisation giving some degree of justification.					
Can the pupil:					
i	Argue clearly with a logical flow of ideas?				
ii	Recognise and define subtle patterns in information?				
iii	Recognise and define subtle patterns in arrangements or sequences of shapes or numbers?				
iv	Suggest rules which connect sets or sequences of numbers?				
v	Use a range of techniques of handling data to justify conclusions?				
vi	Reason with some precision in a problem or puzzle context?				
vii	Test simple generalisations or hypotheses by use of examples extrapolated from given data or information?				
viii	Sensibly discuss conclusions in order to justify or substantiate opinions?				

Ma 2/5a

SERIES **I**

Use an appropriate non-calculator method to multiply or divide two numbers

1 Calculate (showing your working):

472 × 24

2 Calculate (showing your working):

217 × 93

3 Calculate (showing your working):

345 ÷ 23

4 Calculate (showing your working):

592 ÷ 16

5 A group of 326 people each paid £17 to go on a camping trip. How much money was paid altogether? (Show your working.)

6 A sum of £285 was shared equally among 15 classes to spend on library books. How much did each class receive? (Show your working.)

7 Calculate how many buses are needed to take 223 people on a trip, if each bus holds 47 people. (Show your working.)

8 Calculate the cost in pounds and pence of buying 295 cans of Cola for a school party if each can costs 33p. (Show your working.)

9 Work these out in your head. Write down the answers.

a 50 × 20 =

b 200 × 30 =

c 30 × 70 =

d 300 × 90 =

10 Work these out in your head. Write down the answers.

a 400 ÷ 20 =

b 6000 ÷ 20 =

c 8000 ÷ 200 =

d 8000 ÷ 40 =

11 Write the correct numbers in the empty boxes.

a

| 50 | × 200 → | | ÷ 40 → | |

b

| | × 50 → | | ÷ 20 → | 100 |

c

| | × 5 → | 1000 | ÷ 20 → | |

Name **Date**

Find fractions or percentages of quantities

1

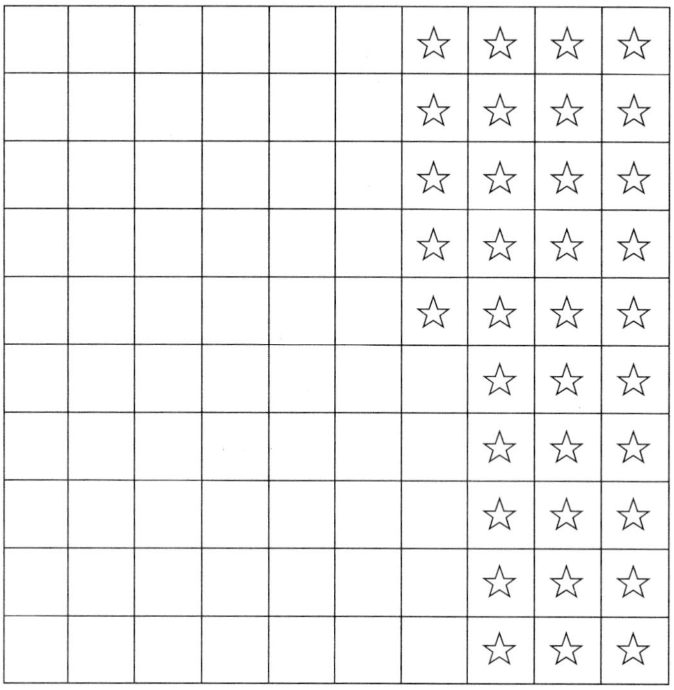

a What fraction of the squares contains stars? (Write it in its lowest terms.) ☐

b What percentage of the squares is empty? ☐ %

c What percentage of the squares contains stars? ☐ %

2 Calculate $\frac{2}{5}$ of 800 grams. ☐ g

3 Calculate 45% of 40 kg. ☐ kg

4 Write $2\frac{1}{2}$% as a fraction in its lowest terms. ☐

5 What is 100% of £1? £ ☐

6 Calculate $\frac{5}{8}$ of £176. £ ☐

7 Calculate 22% of £99. £ ☐

8 In a class of 35 pupils, two-fifths are boys.

   a How many boys are there?

   b How many girls are there?

9 What is 90p as a percentage of £2.40?

%

10 A woman gave an amount of money to local charities. She gave:

20% of the money to the hospital
50% of the money to a playgroup
and £30 to an animal welfare group.
How much money did she give away altogether?

£

11 In June, it rained on 12 days.

   a What fraction of the whole month was rainy?

   b What percentage of the whole month was dry?

%

12 Look at these offers and tick the one that is the best value.

   ☐ Cassettes: £2 off if you spend £8

   ☐ Chocolate: 19p off a 70p bar

   ☐ Books: £3 off if you spend £10

1 Write these numbers correct to 1 decimal place.

   a 6.371 ⟶ ⬭

   b 2.946 ⟶ ⬭

   c 0.882 ⟶ ⬭

2 Write these numbers correct to 3 decimal places.

   a 3.265 71 ⟶ ⬭

   b 8.555 55 ⟶ ⬭

   c 0.0026 31 ⟶ ⬭

3 Write these numbers correct to 1 significant figure.

   a 3758 ⟶ ⬭

   b 39.23 ⟶ ⬭

   c 0.026 ⟶ ⬭

4 Write these numbers correct to 3 significant figures.

   a 3293.15 ⟶ ⬭

   b 3.027 ⟶ ⬭

   c 0.001 23 ⟶ ⬭

5 a Use a trial and improvement method to find the amount each person would get if £500 were shared equally among three people.

   b The amount correct to 3 significant figures is ⬭

6 a Use a trial and improvement method to find the length of one side of a small square table if the area is 2000 cm^2.

   b The length of the side, correct to 3 decimal places, is ⬭

1 Complete these.

    a 10 mm = ( ) cm   **e** 1000 g = ( ) kg

    b 1 m = ( ) cm   **f** 1000 kg = ( ) tonne

    c 1 km = ( ) m   **g** 1000 ml = ( ) litre

    d 1 m = ( ) mm

2 Complete these.

    a 32.9 kg = ( ) g

    b 16.5 kg = ( ) kg and ( ) g

    c 2184 g = ( ) kg

    d 2.4 tonnes = ( ) kg

    e 0.45 kg = ( ) g

    f 1.5 litres = ( ) ml

    g 0.023 litres = ( ) ml

3 Complete these.

    a 6.3 km = ( ) m

    b 7842 m = ( ) km

    c 0.225 m = ( ) cm

    d 500 cm = ( ) m

    e 6233 mm = ( ) m

    f 54 cm = ( ) mm

    g 0.4 cm = ( ) mm

4 Add 250 cm and 2.8 metres. Give the answer in metres.

( ) m

5 Add 2 kg 120 g and 0.5 kg. Give the answer in kilograms.

( ) kg

6 From 2.2 litres subtract 1500 ml. Give the answer in litres.

( ) litres

7 From 0.9 metres subtract 350 mm. Give the answer in millimetres.

( ) mm

8 Complete these.

a 12 inches = ( ) foot

d ( ) ounces = 1 pound

b ( ) feet = 1 yard

e 14 pounds = ( ) stone

c 1760 yards = ( ) mile

f ( ) pints = 1 gallon

9 Ring the correct answer to each of these.

a	1 inch is about	1 cm	$2\frac{1}{2}$ cm	2 cm	2 mm
b	1 foot is about	10 cm	12 cm	20 cm	30 cm
c	1 yard is about	90 cm	36 cm	70 cm	100 cm
d	1 mile is about	1 km	$1\frac{1}{2}$ km	3 km	5 km
e	1 ounce is about	10 g	20 g	30 g	40 g
f	1 pound is about	1 kg	$\frac{1}{4}$ kg	$\frac{1}{2}$ kg	$\frac{3}{4}$ kg
g	1 stone is about	4 kg	5 kg	6 kg	10 kg
h	1 pint is about	400 ml	600 ml	700 ml	800 ml
i	1 gallon is about	$2\frac{1}{2}$ litres	$3\frac{1}{2}$ litres	$4\frac{1}{2}$ litres	$5\frac{1}{2}$ litres

10

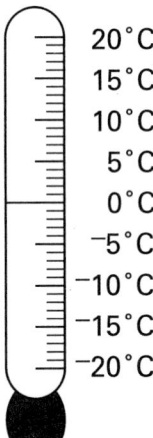

20°C
15°C
10°C
5°C
0°C
−5°C
−10°C
−15°C
−20°C

a Write these temperatures in order, highest first.

10°C   −15°C   6°C   0°C   −10°C

highest [ ] [ ] [ ] [ ] [ ] lowest

b Complete this chart.

starting temperature	change in temperature	finishing temperature
10°C	falls 3°C	
3°C	falls 5°C	
−7°C	rises 3°C	
−6°C	falls 4°C	
−2°C	rises 8°C	

11 In a quiz you start with 8 points.
You add 2 points for a correct answer. ✔
You subtract 1 point for a wrong answer. ✗

How many points
do these
people end up with?

Name	Question number										Score
	1	2	3	4	5	6	7	8	9	10	
Jane	✔	✔	✗	✗	✗	✗	✗	✗	✗	✔	points
Tom	✗	✗	✗	✔	✔	✔	✔	✗	✔	✗	points
Sonia	✔	✗	✔	✗	✗	✗	✗	✔	✗	✗	points
Kim	✗	✔	✗	✔	✗	✔	✗	✗	✔	✗	points
Ali	✗	✗	✔	✔	✔	✔	✗	✗	✔	✗	points

1 This sequence of dot patterns shows triangular numbers. Draw the next three patterns in the sequence.

The 8th number in the sequence is ⬭

2 Draw the next pattern of dots in this sequence.

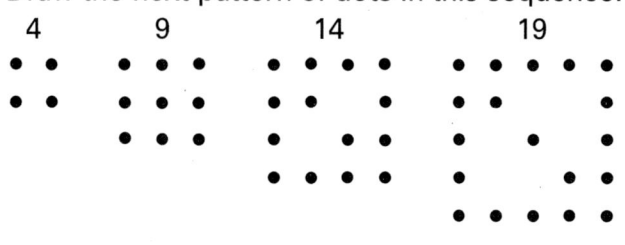 

The 8th number in the sequence is ⬭

3 Write the sequence of the first five numbers following the instructions.

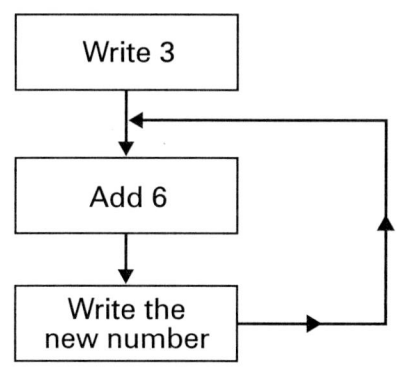 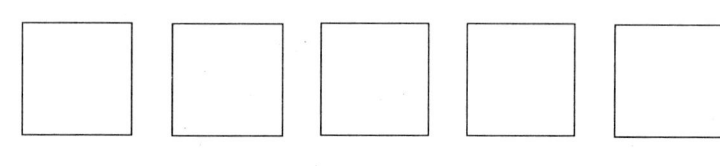

4 Underline the sequence which is formed using this rule:

| Start with 5, add 4 each time. |

| 5 | 9 | 14 | 20 | 27 |

or

| 5 | 9 | 13 | 17 | 21 |

5 Ring the prime numbers in this sequence.

9   13   17   25   29   33

6 Write down the sequence of the first five numbers using this rule.

Start with 4. Multiply by 2 and add 1.

7 Write the sequence of the first five equivalent fractions formed using this rule.

Start with $\frac{2}{3}$. Multiply the numerator and the denominator by 2.

8 Write down the sequence of five numbers given by this BASIC program.

```
10   FOR NUMBER = 1 TO 5
20   PRINT NUMBER + 2
30   NEXT NUMBER
40   END
```

9 Write down the sequence of five numbers given by this BASIC program.

```
10   FOR NUMBER = 1 TO 5
20   PRINT NUMBER * NUMBER
30   NEXT NUMBER
40   END
```

The square root of 25 is

10 Write down the sequence of five numbers given by this BASIC program.

```
10   FOR NUMBER = 1 TO 5
20   PRINT NUMBER * NUMBER * NUMBER
30   NEXT NUMBER
40   END
```

The cube root of 125 is

11 Write down the next three equivalent fractions in this sequence.

$$\frac{2}{5} \qquad \frac{6}{15} \qquad \frac{18}{45}$$

Ma 3/5b
SERIES **I**

Express a simple function symbolically

1 Write a formula for the cost (c) in pence of 2 kg of apples at x pence per kilogram.

2 A girl has £e. She spends £f. Write a formula for the amount (a) in £s she has left.

3 Two tapes are x metres and y metres long. Laid together, their total length is 25 metres. Write a formula linking x and y.

4 Chairs are arranged in r rows. The number of chairs in each row is c. There are 36 chairs altogether. Write a formula linking r and c.

5 Emma's age is e years. Tariq is three years older than Emma. Write a formula to express Tariq's age (t) in years.

6 A group of d children share c sweets among themselves. How many sweets does each child get?

7 I think of a number n, add 3, then multiply the answer by n. The result is p. Write a formula linking these facts.

8 Find the function linking these values of x and y.

x		y
2	→	6
4	→	8
6	→	10
8	→	12
10	→	14

9 Write the functions linking the values of x and y.

	Input			Output	Function
a	x	× 2	− 5	y	
b	x	− 3	× 4	y	
c	x	× 5	÷ 2	y	

10 Write an equation to represent these amounts which balance.

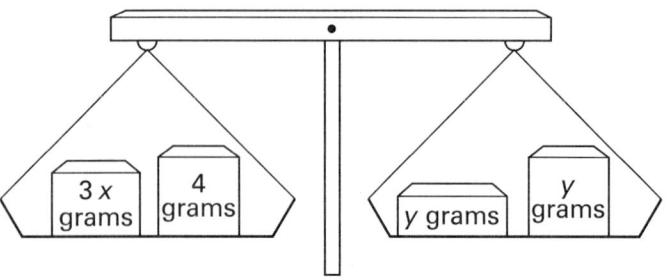

┌─────────────────┐
│   │
│   =   │
│   │
└─────────────────┘

11 The perimeter (p) of a rectangle is given by the formula $p = 2(w + l)$.

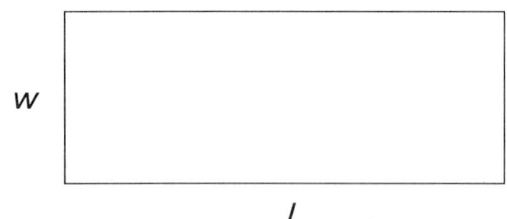

a If w is 3 cm and l is 5 cm then $p = $ ( ) cm

b If p is 24 cm and w is 4 cm then $l = $ ( ) cm

12 Write a formula for the perimeter (p) of this shape.

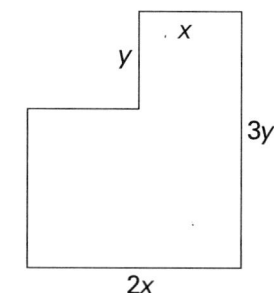

┌──────────────────────┐
│   │
│   │
└──────────────────────┘

13

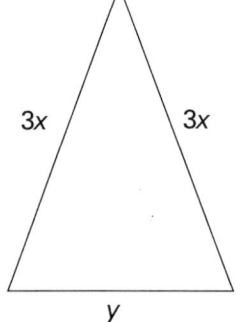

a Write a formula for the perimeter (p) of this triangle.

┌──────────────────────────────────┐
│   │
│   │
└──────────────────────────────────┘

b What is the perimeter if x is 2 cm and y is 2 cm?

┌──────────────┐
│   │ cm
└──────────────┘

14 We can convert temperatures from degrees Fahrenheit (F) to degrees Celsius (C) using this formula:

$F = \frac{9}{5}C + 32$

If the temperature is 22°C,
what is it in °F,
to the nearest degree?

 °F

You need: ruler, protractor, compasses, scissors, sellotape

1 What is the length of this line, in millimetres?

_____ ( ) mm

2 Measure each angle to the nearest degree.

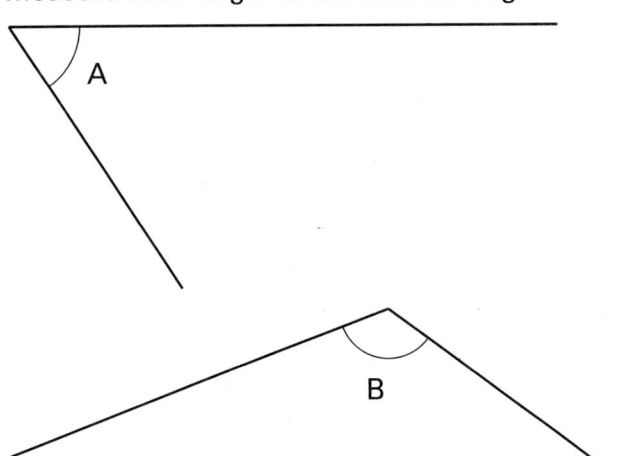

Angle A = ( )°

Angle B = ( )°

Angle C = ( )°

Angle D = ( )°

Angle E = ( )°

Angle F = ( )°

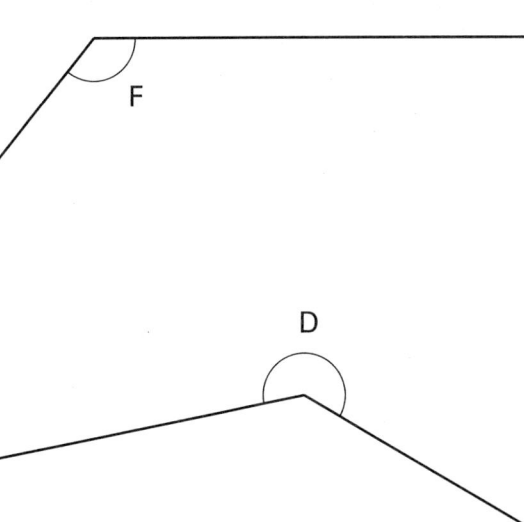

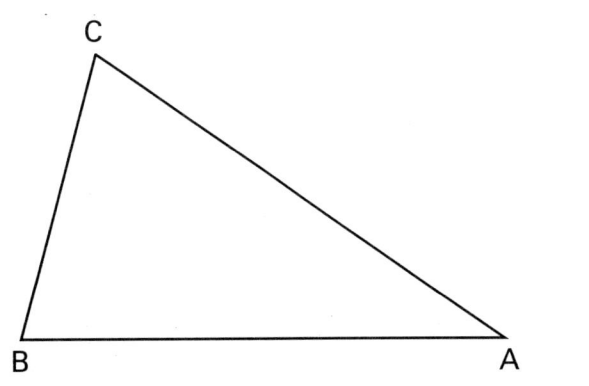

3 Measure the sides and angles of this triangle.

a Length AB is ( ) cm

b Length BC is ( ) cm

c Length AC is ( ) cm

d Angle CAB is ( )°

e Angle ABC is ( )°

f Angle BCA is ( )°

4 In the space, draw these angles.

   a   A = 37°

   b   B = 124°

   c   C = 213°

> Mark each angle with the letter, an arc and the number of degrees, e.g.
>
>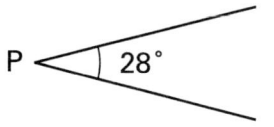
>
> P   28°

5 Use this space to construct the triangle XYZ in which

XY is 6.3 cm
∠ZXY is 42°
∠XYZ is 47°.

   a   Length XZ is (   ) cm

   b   Length YZ is (   ) cm

6 Use strong paper or card to construct a square-based pyramid. Use a net like this with the given lengths and angles.

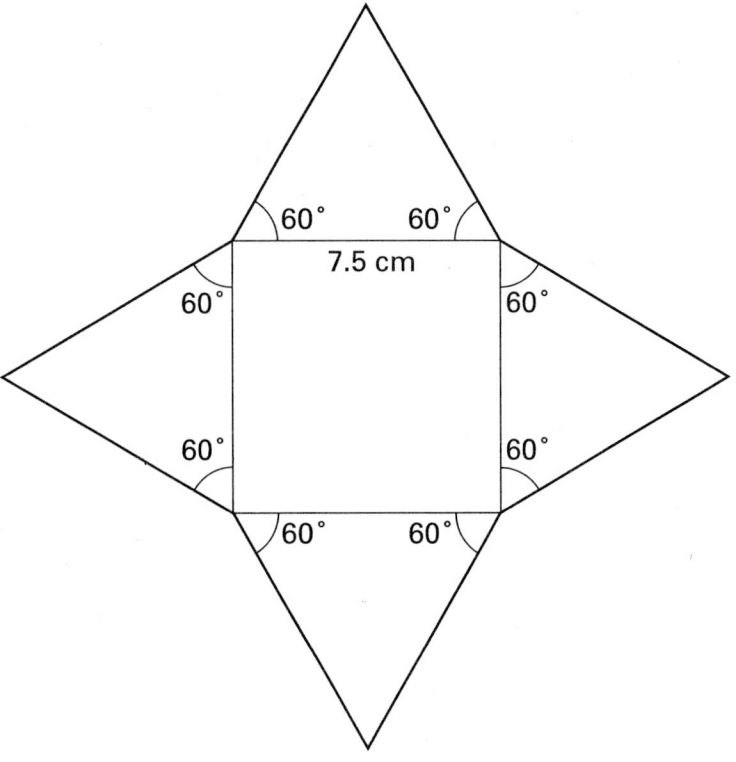

7 Use strong paper or card to construct a triangular prism like this, with the given lengths and angles.

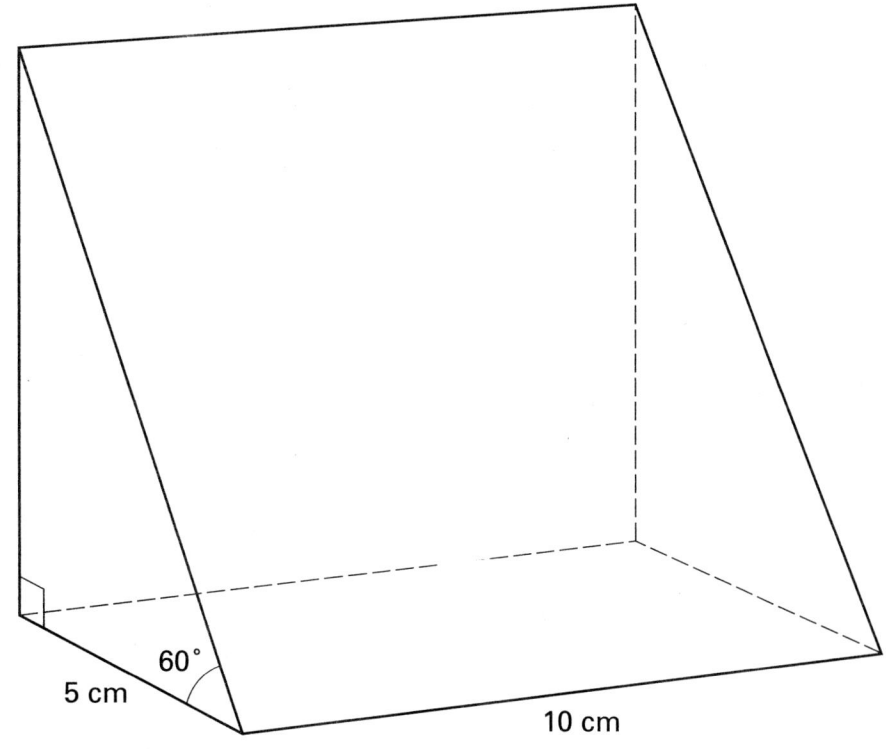

1 Write down the sizes of the three other angles in this diagram.

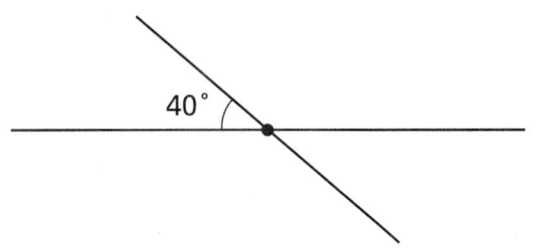

2 Mark the angles that are equal to the angle marked with a star.

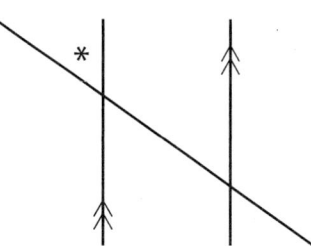

3 Two angles which add up to 180°

are ⬭

and ⬭ .

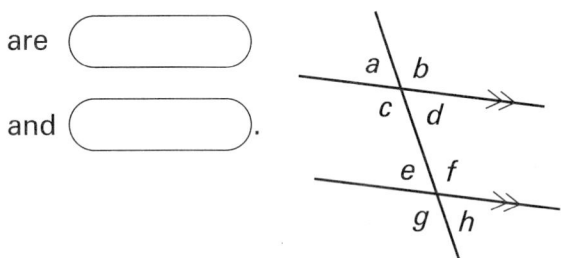

4

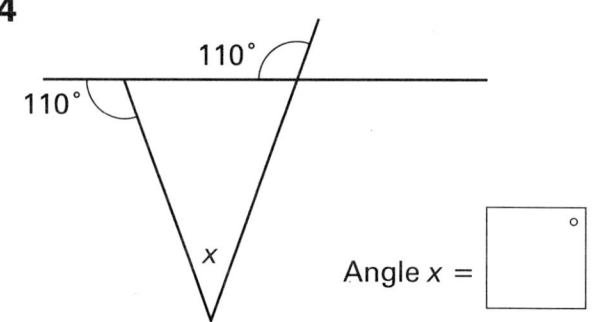

Angle x = ▢ °

5

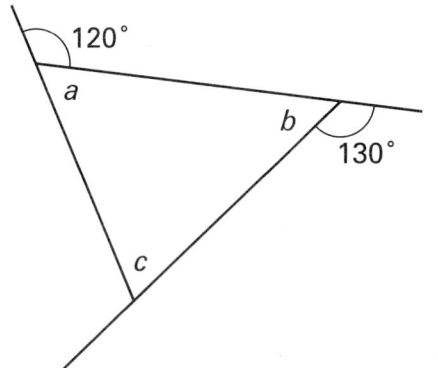

a Angle a = ⬭ °

b Angle b = ⬭ °

c Angle c = ⬭ °

6

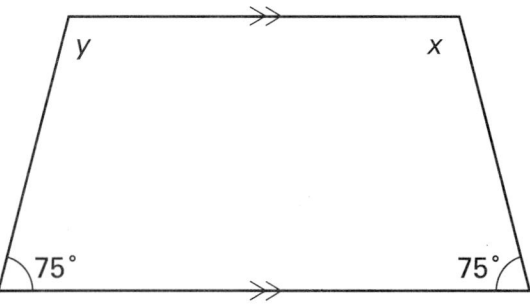

a Angle x = ⬭ °

b Angle y = ⬭ °

7

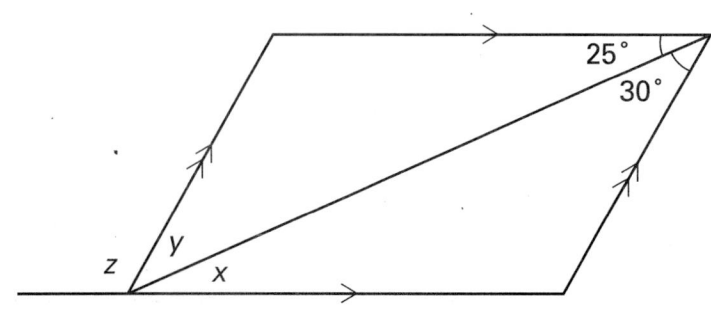

a Angle x = ⬭ °

b Angle y = ⬭ °

c Angle z = ⬭ °

Name   **Date**

Use properties of shape to justify explanations

8 Tick two adjacent angles.

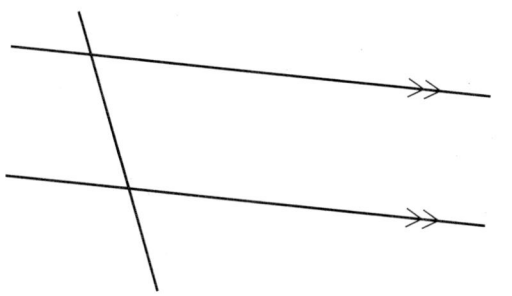

9 Tick two vertically opposite angles.

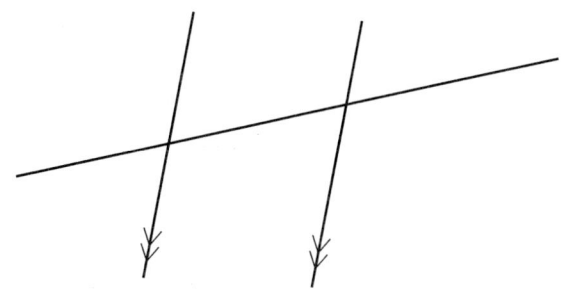

10 Tick two corresponding angles.

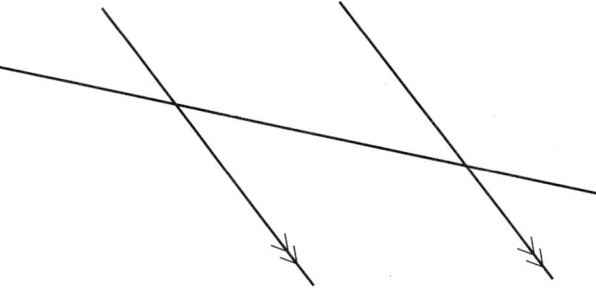

11 Tick two alternate angles.

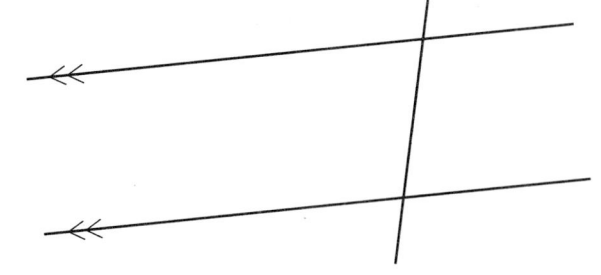

12

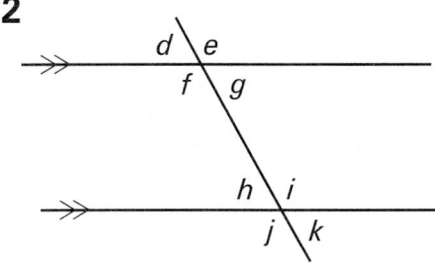

d e
f g

h i
j k

a Two adjacent angles are ◯ and ◯ .

b Two vertically opposite angles are ◯ and ◯ .

c Two corresponding angles are ◯ and ◯ .

d Two alternate angles are ◯ and ◯ .

13 Angle x in the rectangle = ◯ °

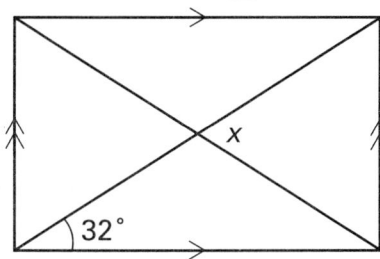

32°

x

14 Angle x = ◯ °

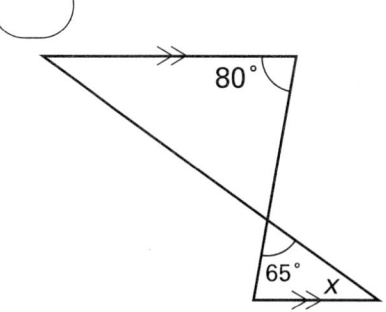

80°

65° x

15 Angle x = ◯ °

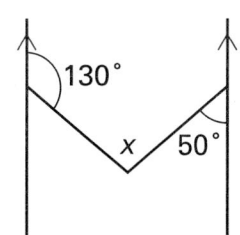

130°

x 50°

16 Angle x = ◯ °

x

65°

Mathscheck

Ma 4/5b
SERIES I

Name

Date

Use properties of shape to justify explanations

17 A B C D E S H J P

Which of these letters have

a reflective but not rotational symmetry

b rotational but not reflective symmetry

c reflective and rotational symmetry

d neither reflective nor rotational symmetry?

18 A square has ( ) lines of reflective symmetry
and rotational symmetry of order ( ) .

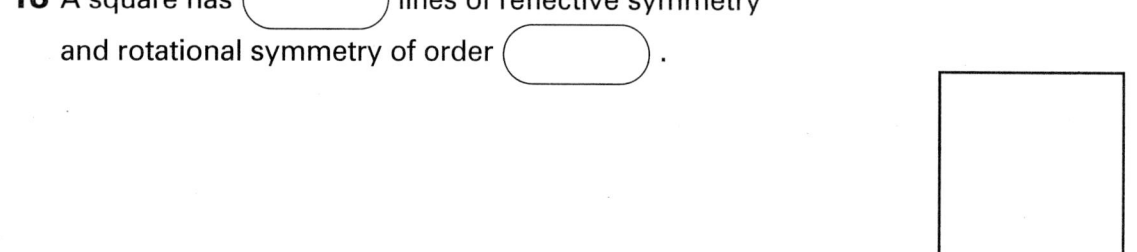

19 A parallelogram has ( ) lines of reflective symmetry

and rotational symmetry of order ( ) .

20 Draw a shape with rotational symmetry
of order 3.

21 A square-based pyramid has [ ] planes
of symmetry.

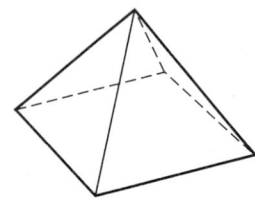

22 This shape has [ ] planes of symmetry.

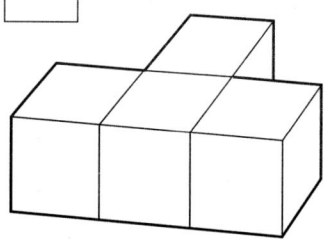

Name   **Date**

Use networks to solve problems

1 Travelling only across (→) or down (↓), how many different routes are there from A to B?

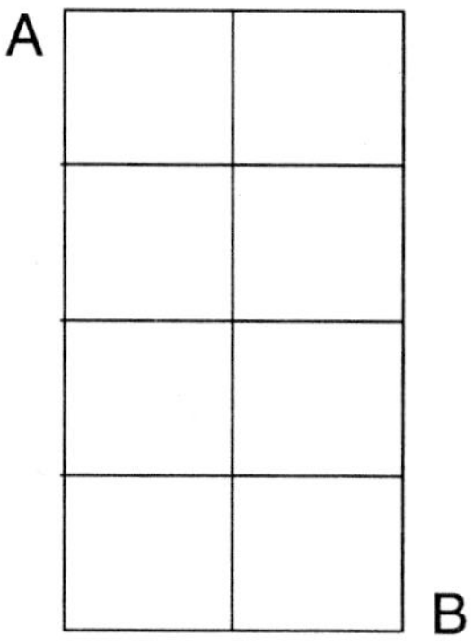

A

B

[ ] routes

2 This grid is traversable.   Show how on this dotted grid.

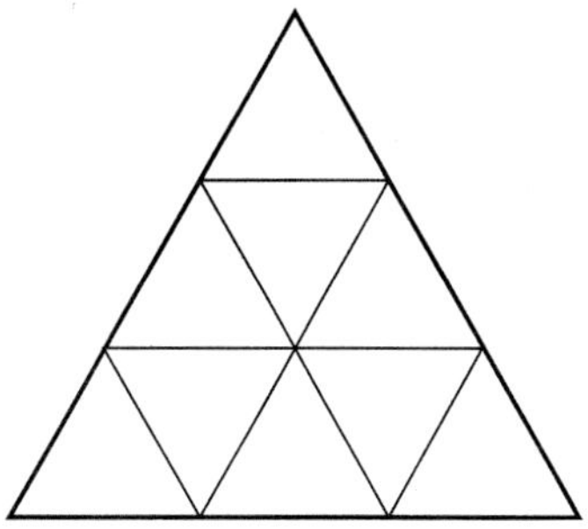

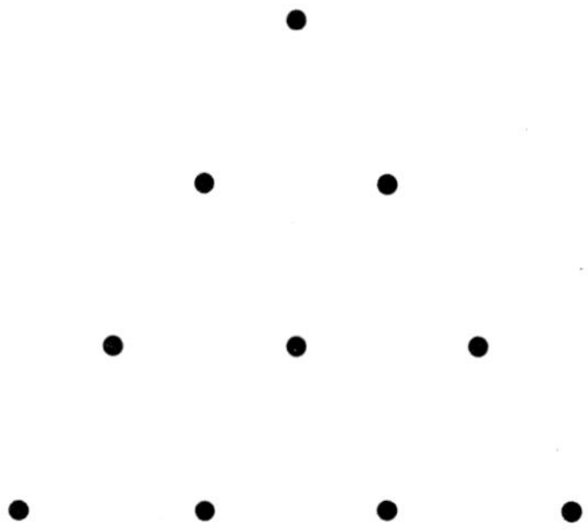

3 Five people met and they all shook hands with each other. Draw a network to show all the handshakes.

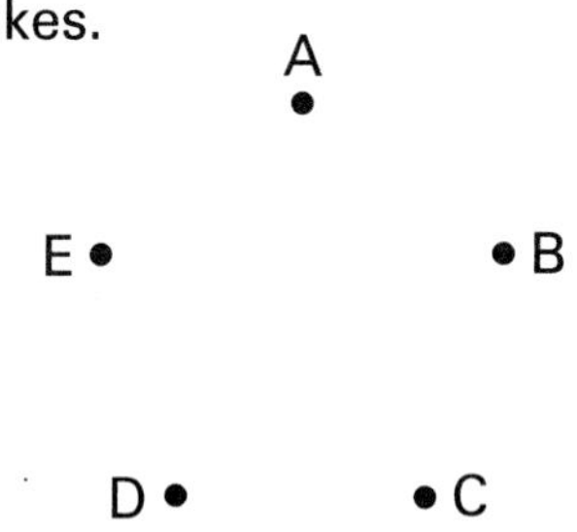

A

E •   • B

The total number of handshakes is [ ]

D •   • C

4 The postman's van starts and finishes at A. He visits each place only once and does not travel along the same road twice.

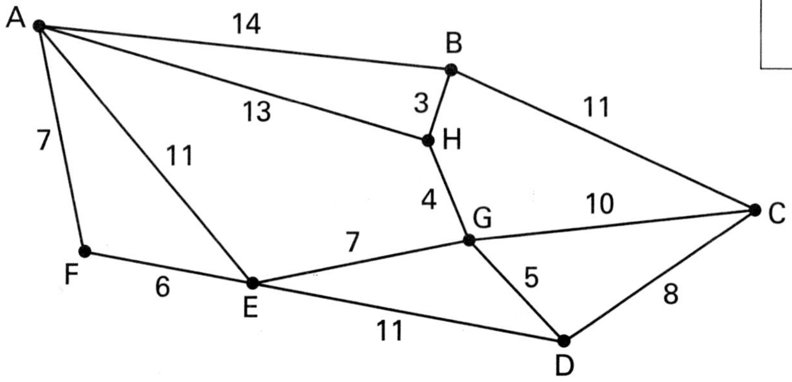

The **shortest** route he would take is

A →

The length of the shortest route

is ( ) km

A

14

B

13   3   11

7   11   H

4   G   10   C

7

F   6   E   5

11   8

D

1 Area is [ ] cm².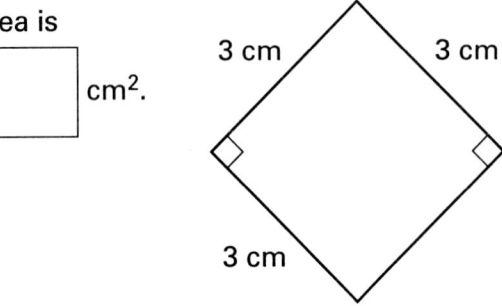

3 cm 3 cm

3 cm

2 Area is [ ] cm².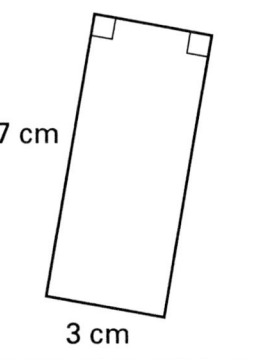

7 cm

3 cm

3 Area is [ ] cm².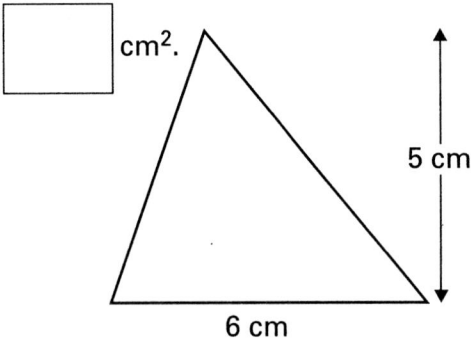

5 cm

6 cm

4 Area is [ ] cm².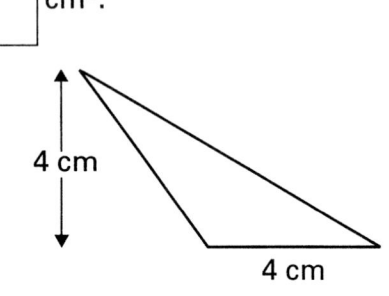

4 cm

4 cm

5 Area is [ ] cm².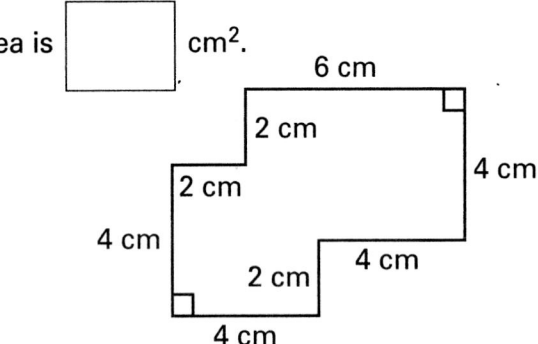

6 cm

2 cm

2 cm

4 cm

4 cm

2 cm   4 cm

4 cm

6 Area is [ ] cm².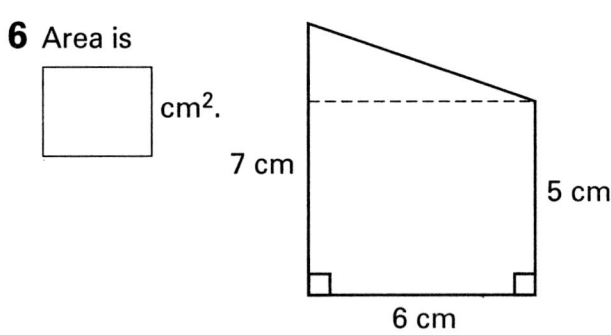

7 cm

6 cm

5 cm

7 Area is [ ] cm².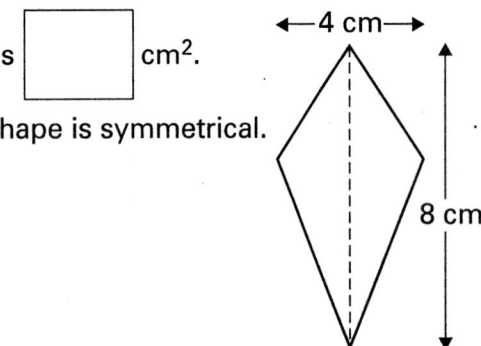

The shape is symmetrical.

←4 cm→

8 cm

8 Area is [ ] cm².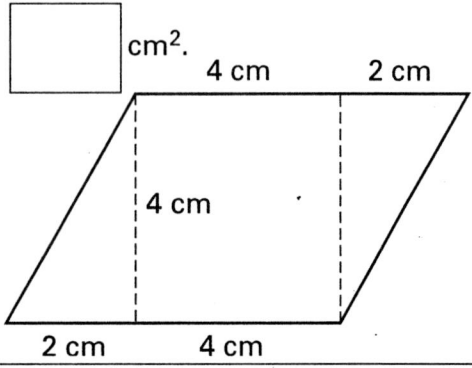

4 cm   2 cm

4 cm

2 cm   4 cm

9 Area of frame is [ ] cm².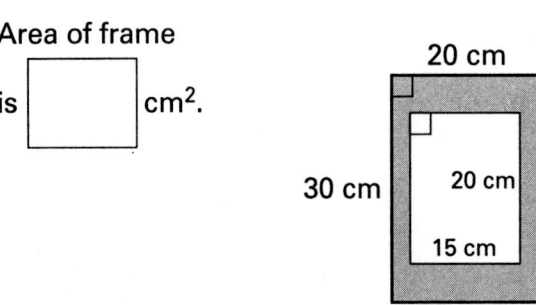

20 cm

30 cm

20 cm

15 cm

10 Area of frame is [ ] cm².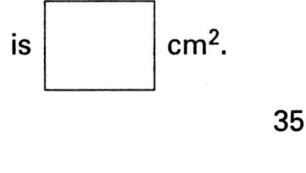

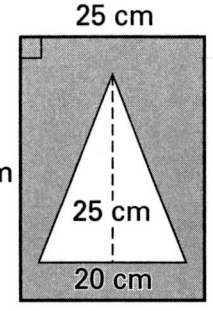

25 cm

35 cm

25 cm

20 cm

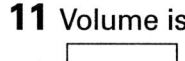
11 Volume is ▢ cm³.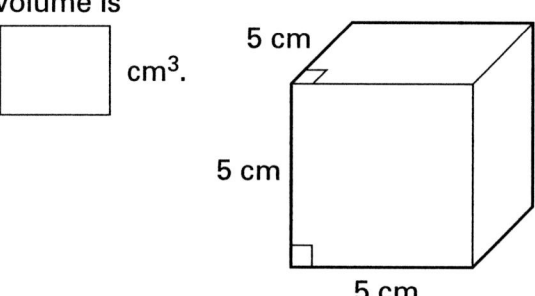

5 cm
5 cm
5 cm

12 Volume is ▢ cm³.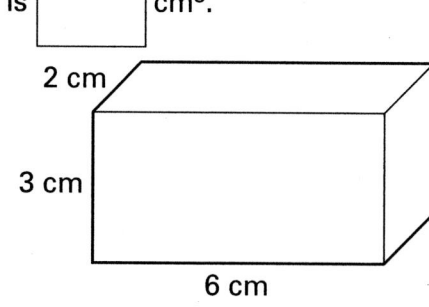

2 cm
3 cm
6 cm

13 Volume is ▢ cm³.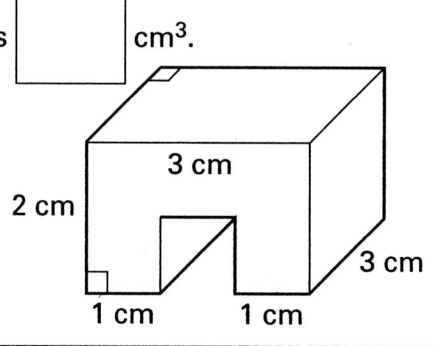

3 cm
2 cm
3 cm
1 cm   1 cm

14 Volume is ▢ cm³.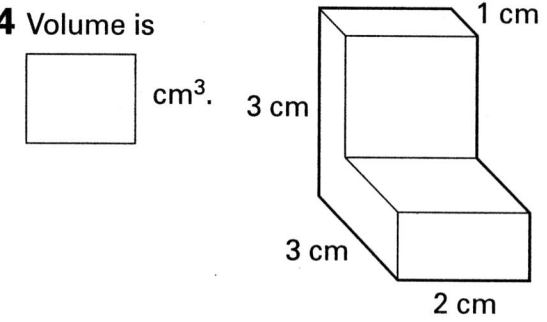

1 cm
3 cm
3 cm
2 cm

15 Volume is ▢ cm³.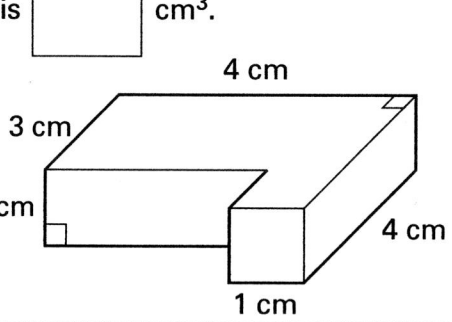

4 cm
3 cm
1 cm
1 cm
4 cm

16 Volume is ▢ cm³.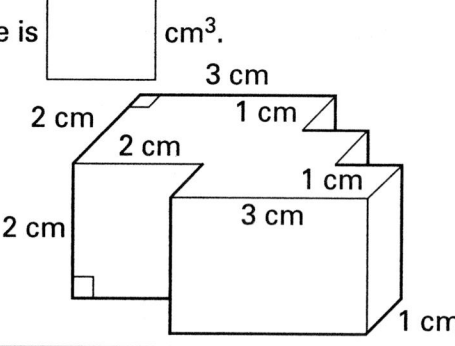

3 cm
2 cm   1 cm
2 cm
1 cm
2 cm   3 cm
1 cm

17 Volume is ▢ cm³.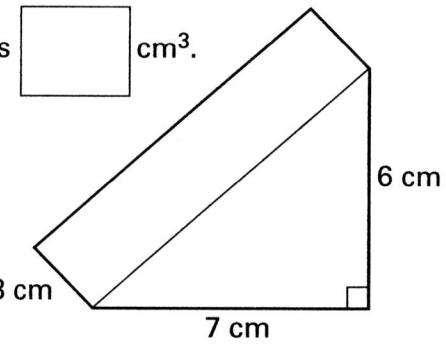

6 cm
3 cm
7 cm

18 Volume is ▢ cm³.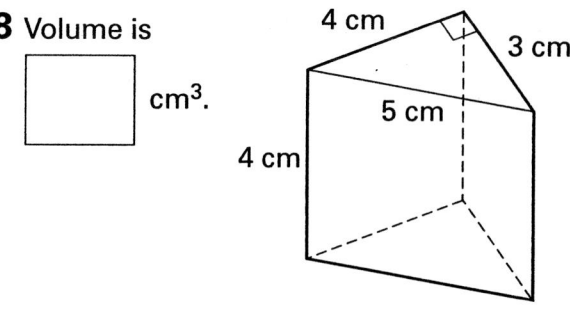

4 cm
3 cm
5 cm
4 cm

19 The total height of the shape is 8 cm.
The volume of the whole shape
is ▢ cm³.

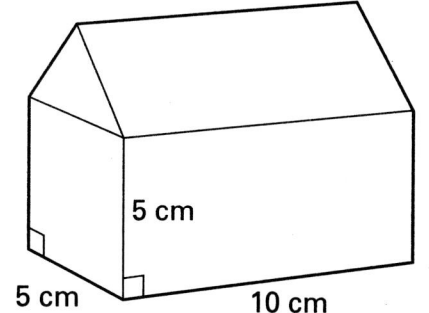

5 cm
5 cm   10 cm

Use a computer database package and have your work
checked after each activity.

Tick when completed.

1 Set up a database file to hold 12 records, each containing 4 fields.   ◯

2 Enter this data about volcanoes then save the file onto a floppy disc.   ◯

Record	Field 1	Field 2	Field 3	Field 4
	Name	Country	Height in metres	Condition
1	Fujiyama	Japan	3778	extinct
2	Paricutin	Mexico	2774	dormant
3	Cotopaxi	Ecuador	5978	active
4	Mauna Loa	Hawaii	4168	active
5	Erebus	Antarctica	4023	active
6	Etna	Sicily	3287	active
7	Nyiregongo	Congo	3470	active
8	Demavend	Iran	5366	extinct
9	Kilimanjaro	Tanzania	5889	dormant
10	Popocatapetl	Mexico	5452	active
11				
12				

3 Add this record to the database file and save it again.

Record   11 | Wrangell | USA | 4269 | active | ◯

4 Sort the records into alphabetic order.   ◯

5 Sort the records into height order, tallest first.   ◯

6 Name the highest active volcano.

7 Name two active volcanoes higher than 5000 metres.   a

                                                               b

1 A weekend survey of the colours of 50 people's socks produced this data.

> black black blue white green green red grey grey grey
> brown black black brown red white green white brown black
> blue white white brown grey black blue green black white
> brown grey black blue black white black blue grey brown
> brown black white black green black brown white black white

a Design and draw a recording sheet for collecting the data.

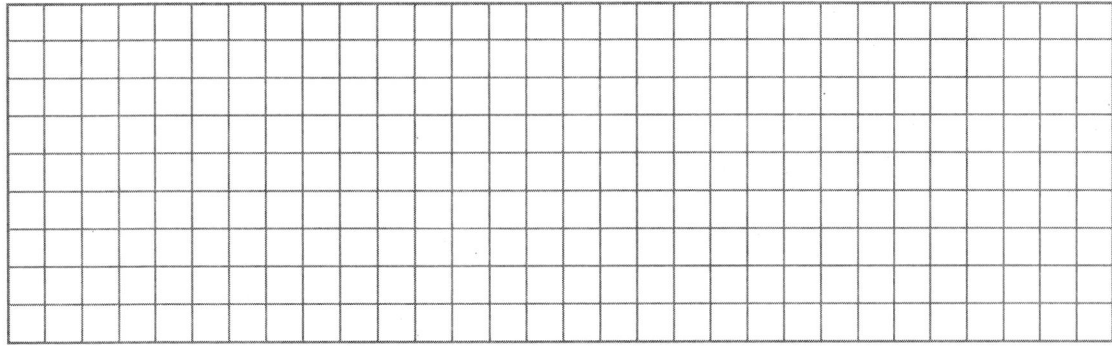

b Write down two pieces of information shown by the collected data.

2 Design an observation sheet on which to record data about the number of words in each sentence on one page of an encyclopaedia.

a Use it to carry out the collection of data.

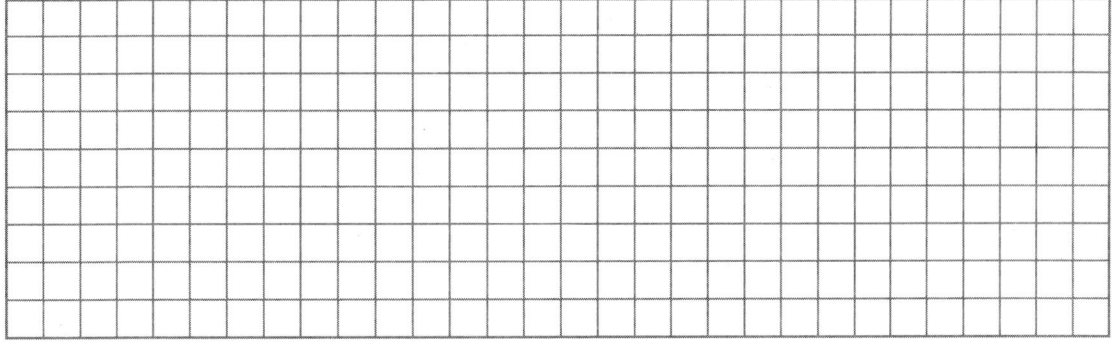

b Write down two pieces of information shown by the data.

3 This data shows the results of a 'Welly throwing' competition.
The distances are in metres.

16.2	14.9	15.4	15.6	15.3	15.9	15.8	15.2	15.7
16.0	15.5	15.2	15.7	15.5	15.9	16.0	15.6	15.1
16.0	17.6	15.9	15.2	17.0	15.5	16.3	15.9	14.7
15.6	15.8	14.7	15.4	15.8	15.4	15.8	15.0	14.3
15.1	15.0	15.6	15.4	15.7	15.0	15.8	15.6	17.0

a Draw and complete a frequency table of the results using four equal class intervals.

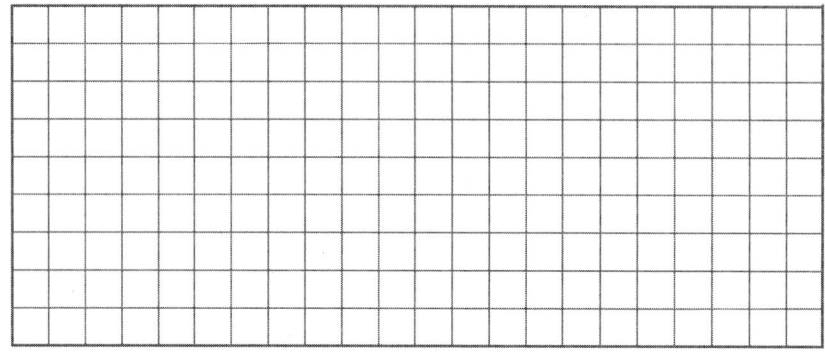

b Draw a graph of the results.

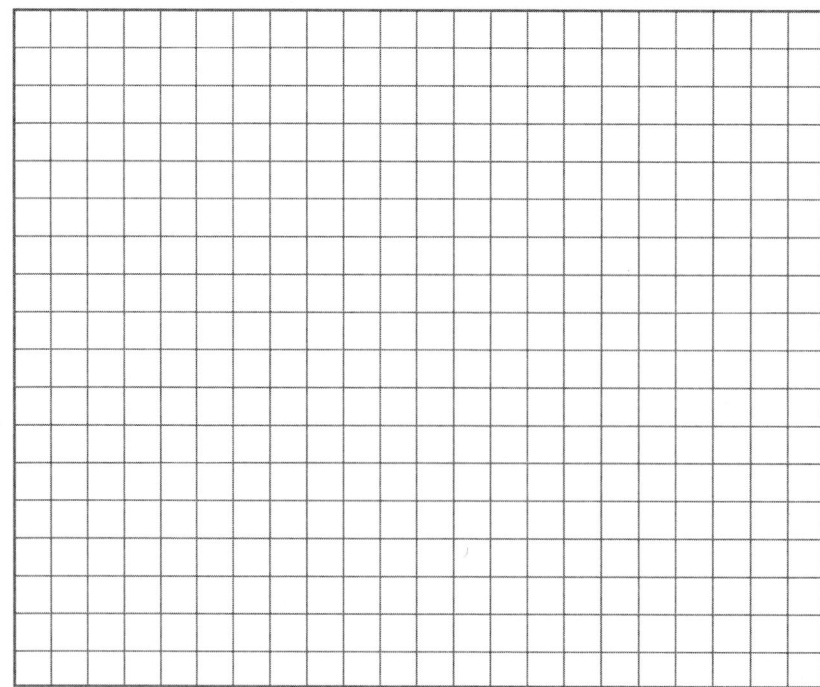

c Write down two pieces of information shown by the graph or frequency table.

1 In a survey, 36 people were asked to taste four drinks and say which they preferred. The results were:

apple juice   9
orange juice   15
lime juice   3
pineapple juice   9

Construct a pie chart from the data.

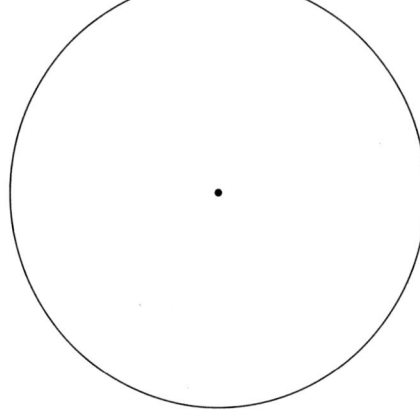

2 Construct a pie chart from the information shown in the bar chart.

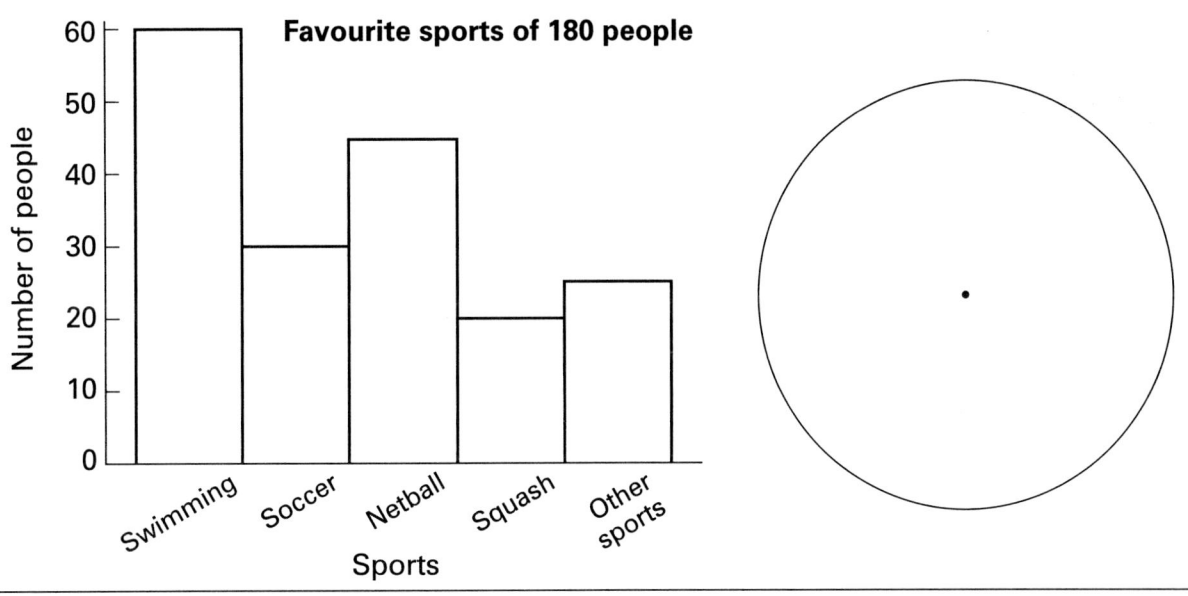

3 In a survey, 24 people were asked to name their favourite colour from a choice of four. This pie chart was drawn from the results.

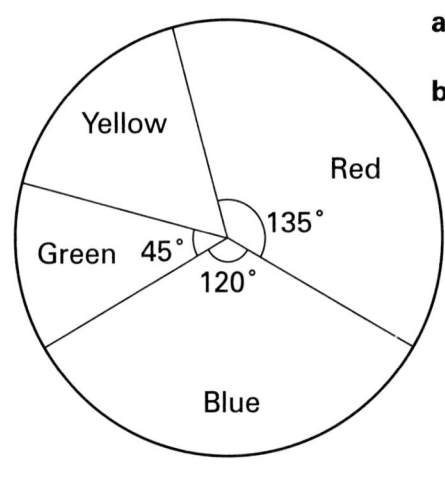

a The angle for the yellow section is [   ] °.

b Write down the numbers of people who chose each colour.

red   ⟶ (   )

blue   ⟶ (   )

green   ⟶ (   )

yellow   ⟶ (   )

4 This is a graph showing the relation between litres and gallons.

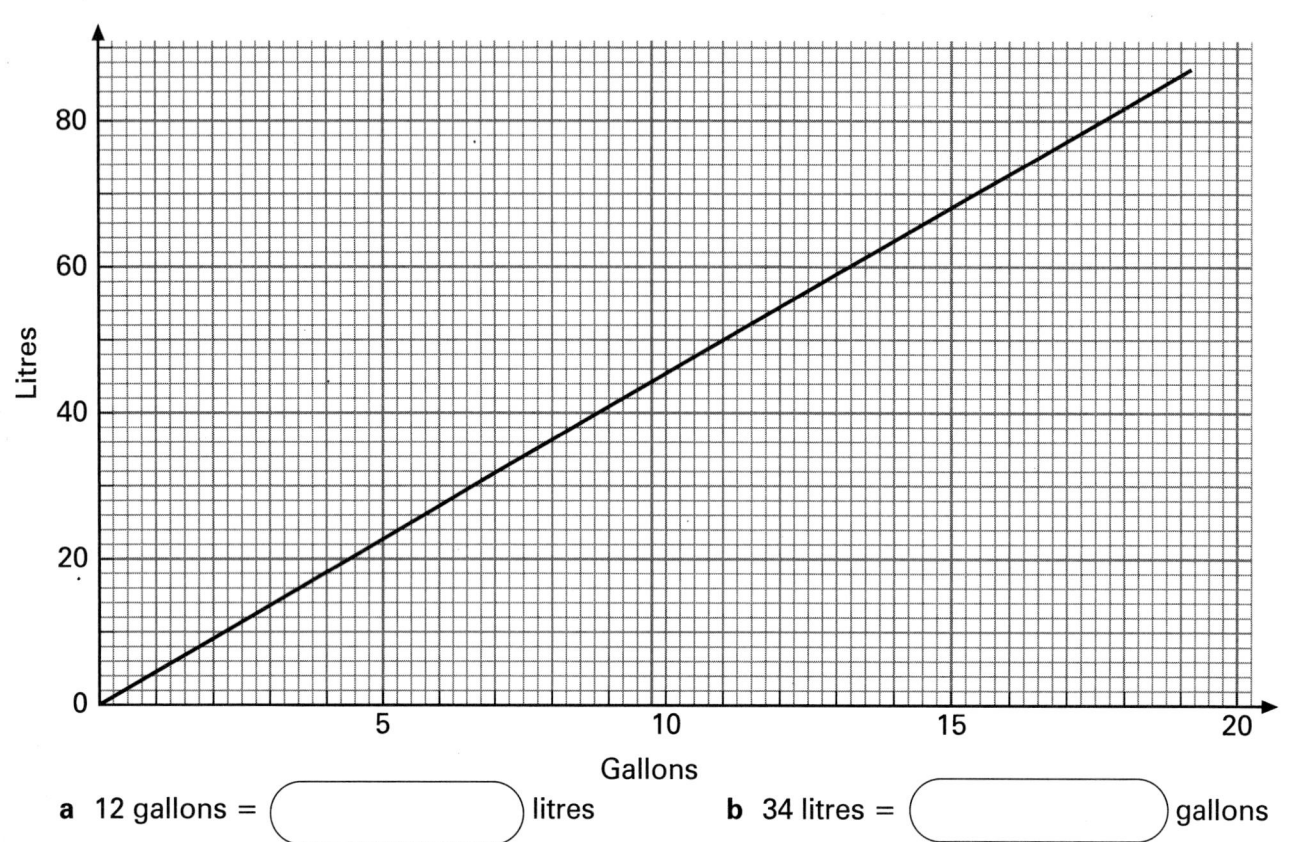

a 12 gallons = (_____) litres   **b** 34 litres = (_____) gallons

5 Draw a conversion graph to convert between miles and kilometres.

1 mile = 1·61 km and 1 km = 0·62 miles

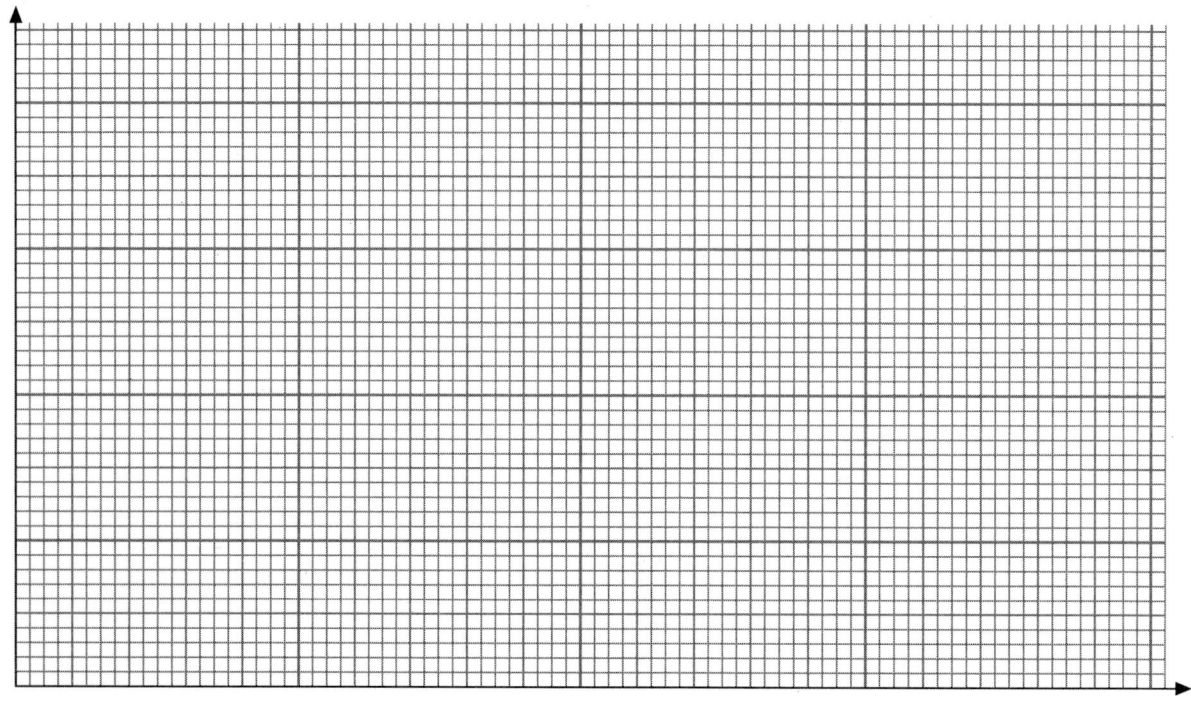

1 Write T for true or F for false in each box.

The spinner is spun 10 times.

RED

BLUE

a There will **always** be some reds and some blues.

b There will **never** be 10 reds in a row.

c There will be **exactly** five reds and five blues.

d There will **usually** be at least one red.

e There will **usually** be at least one blue.

f There **might** be different numbers of reds and blues.

If the experiment is repeated 100 times to give 1000 results:

g There will **usually** be some reds and some blues.

h There will **never** be 100 reds in a row.

i There will be **exactly** 500 reds and 500 blues.

j It is **likely** that there will be **about** 500 reds and 500 blues.

2 Which of these situations would allow you to calculate an exact probability and which would have to be estimated?

Write 'exact' or 'estimate' in each box

a The probability that you will throw a 6 on a normal die

b The probability that the next bird to land in your garden will be a crow

c The probability that it will be sunny tomorrow

d The probability of picking the seven of diamonds from a full pack of cards

3 You can win, lose or draw in a game of chess. Write down two reasons why the probability of winning might **not** be $\frac{1}{3}$.

a

b

4 There are four methods for estimating probabilities.

A	**B**	**C**	**D**
Using the idea of equally likely outcomes	By experiment	By survey	Using data collected earlier
Example: The probability of the spinner stopping on red is $\frac{1}{3}$.	Example: coloured beads in a bag Keep drawing out a bead, recording the result and replacing the bead.	Example: collecting and recording data from observation or by questioning people	Example: look at data kept in such places as schools, hospitals, companies or government offices

Choose the best method (A, B, C or D) for estimating the probability that:

a it will rain in London next Monday

b if you drop a carton of eggs three will break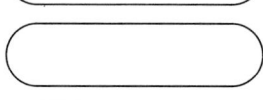

c a single throw of a die will score 2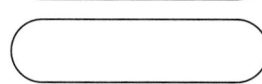

d the next person you see will be wearing red

e the toss of a coin will produce a 'head'.

1 Calculate (showing your working):

329 × 32

2 Calculate (showing your working):

176 × 87

3 Calculate (showing your working):

364 ÷ 28

4 Calculate (showing your working):

782 ÷ 17

5 A shop sold 278 games discs for £13 each. How much money was paid altogether? (Show your working.)

6 A prize of £506 was shared equally among 22 friends. How much did each person receive? (Show your working.)

1 Calculate (showing your working):

2 Calculate (showing your working):

7 A crate holds 24 bottles. How many crates would be needed to carry 332 bottles? (Show your working.)

8 Calculate the cost in pounds and pence of buying 175 burgers for a school party if each burger costs 57p. (Show your working.)

9 Work these out in your head. Write down the answers.

a $30 \times 60 = $

b $300 \times 20 = $

c $40 \times 80 = $

d $400 \times 70 = $

10 Work these out in your head. Write down the answers.

a $600 \div 30 = $

b $4000 \div 50 = $

c $8000 \div 400 = $

d $8000 \div 20 = $

11 Write the correct numbers in the empty boxes.

a

| 40 | $\xrightarrow{\times 300}$ | | $\xrightarrow{\div 60}$ | |

b

| | $\xrightarrow{\times 40}$ | | $\xrightarrow{\div 50}$ | 200 |

c

| | $\xrightarrow{\times 5}$ | 500 | $\xrightarrow{\div 20}$ | |

Mathscheck **Name** **Date**

Ma 2/5b

SERIES II

Find fractions or percentages of quantities

1

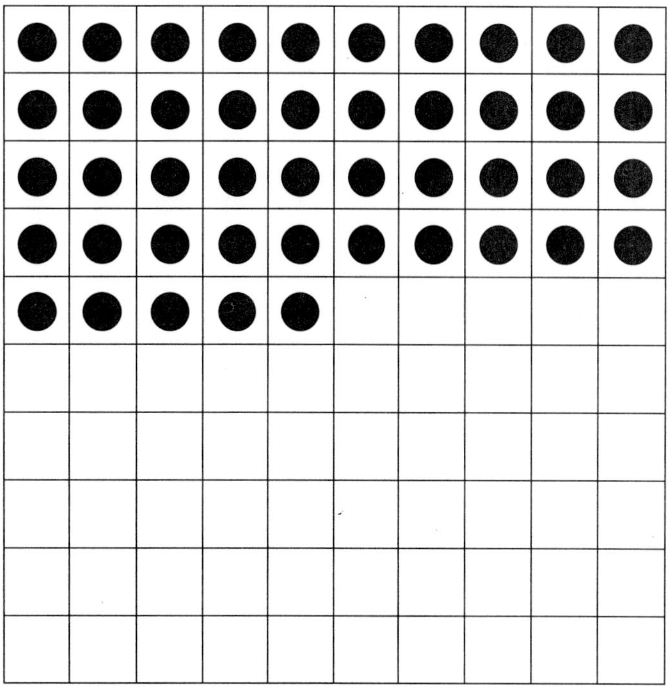

a What fraction of the squares contains dots? (Write it in its lowest terms.) ☐

b What percentage of the squares is empty? ☐ %

c What percentage of the squares contains dots? ☐ %

2 Calculate $\frac{3}{5}$ of £700.

£ ☐

3 Calculate 65% of 80 metres.

☐ m

4 Write $12\frac{1}{2}$ % as a fraction in its lowest terms.

☐

5 What is 100% of 11 km?

☐ km

6 Calculate $\frac{3}{8}$ of 2000 g.

☐ g

7 Calculate 37% of £84.

£ ☐

8 On a shelf of 75 books, three-fifths are fiction.

   a How many fiction books are there?

9 What is 75p as a percentage of £2.50?

   b How many non-fiction books are there?

%

10 A man gave an amount of money to local charities. He gave:

15% of the money to the Old Folks' Home
60% of the money to a Youth Club
and £50 to a local Cats' Home.
How much money did he give away altogether?

£

11 In September, it was sunny on 18 days.

   a What fraction of the whole month was sunny?

   b What percentage of the whole month was not sunny?

%

12 Look at these offers and tick the one that is the best value.

☐ Trainers: £3 off every £12 you spend

☐ Shorts: £1 off every £5 you spend

☐ Shirts: 22% off everything

Name   **Date**

Refine estimations by 'trial and improvement' methods

1 Write these numbers correct to 1 decimal place.

  a 3.542 ⟶ ⬭

  b 12.295 ⟶ ⬭

  c 6.028 ⟶ ⬭

2 Write these numbers correct to 3 decimal places.

  a 2.916 78 ⟶ ⬭

  b 4.545 45 ⟶ ⬭

  c 0.005 61 ⟶ ⬭

3 Write these numbers correct to 1 significant figure.

  a 2089 ⟶ ⬭

  b 32.85 ⟶ ⬭

  c 0.0336 ⟶ ⬭

4 Write these numbers correct to 3 significant figures.

  a 2119.83 ⟶ ⬭

  b 3.926 ⟶ ⬭

  c 0.008 82 ⟶ ⬭

5 a Use a trial and improvement method to find the amount each person would get if £600 were shared equally among seven people.

  b The amount correct to 3 significant figures is ⬭

6 a Use a trial and improvement method to find the length of one side of a small square table if the area is 3000 cm^2.

  b The length of the side, correct to 3 decimal places, is ⬭

Mathscheck

Name

Date

Ma 2/5d
SERIES **II**

Use units in context

1 Complete these.

a 1 litre = ( ) ml

b 100 cm = ( ) m

c 1 cm = ( ) mm

d 1 km = ( ) m

e 1 kg = ( ) g

f 1 tonne = 1000 ( )

g 1000 m = 1 ( )

2 Complete these.

a 33 cm = ( ) mm

b 300 cm = ( ) m

c 2.9 km = ( ) m

d 0.381 m = ( ) cm

e 2222 m = ( ) km

f 1234 mm = ( ) m

g 0.8 cm = ( ) mm

3 Complete these.

a 19.2 kg = ( ) g

b 8.7 kg = ( ) kg and ( ) g

c 1637 g = ( ) kg

d 1.9 tonnes = ( ) kg

e 0.33 kg = ( ) g

f 2.7 litres = ( ) ml

g 0.01 litres = ( ) ml

4 Add 400 ml and 0.85 litres.
Give the answer in litres.

( ) litres

5 Add 0.72 metres and 280 cm.
Give the answer in metres.

( ) m

6 From 1.3 metres subtract 53 cm.
Give the answer in metres.

( ) metres

7 From 1 kg subtract 5 g.
Give the answer in kilograms.

( ) kg

8 Complete these.

   a 1 foot = ( ) inches   **d** 1 pound = ( ) ounces

   b 1 yard = ( ) feet   **e** 1 stone = ( ) pounds

   c 1 mile = ( ) yards   **f** 1 gallon = ( ) pints

9 Ring the correct answer to each of these.

a	1 inch is about	1 cm	2 cm	2·5 cm	3 cm
b	1 foot is about	20 cm	25 cm	30 cm	35 cm
c	1 yard is about	70 cm	80 cm	90 cm	100 cm
d	1 mile is about	5 km	3 km	1·5 km	1 km
e	1 ounce is about	50 g	40 g	30 g	10 g
f	1 pound is about	1 kg	$\frac{3}{4}$ kg	$\frac{1}{2}$ kg	$\frac{1}{4}$ kg
g	1 stone is about	14 kg	4 kg	2 kg	6 kg
h	1 pint is about	1 litre	800 ml	600 ml	400 ml
i	1 gallon is about	4 litres	$4\frac{1}{2}$ litres	5 litres	$5\frac{1}{2}$ litres

10

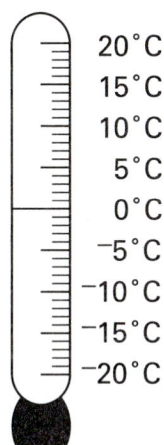

20°C
15°C
10°C
5°C
0°C
−5°C
−10°C
−15°C
−20°C

a Write these temperatures in order, highest first.

    0°C   3°C   −7°C   −10°C   10°C

highest | | | | | | lowest

b Complete this chart.

starting temperature	change in temperature	finishing temperature
2°C	falls 4°C	
10°C	falls 8°C	
−9°C	rises 8°C	
−3°C	falls 7°C	
−6°C	rises 16°C	

11 In a quiz you start with 8 points.
You add 3 points for a correct answer. ✔
You subtract 2 points for a wrong answer. ✘

How many points
do these
people end up with?

Name	Question number										Score
	1	2	3	4	5	6	7	8	9	10	
Eric	✘	✘	✘	✔	✔	✘	✔	✘	✔	✘	points
Al	✔	✔	✘	✘	✘	✘	✘	✔	✔	✘	points
Ella	✘	✔	✘	✘	✘	✔	✘	✔	✘	✘	points
Aziz	✔	✔	✘	✘	✘	✘	✔	✘	✔	✘	points
Mo	✘	✘	✘	✘	✔	✔	✔	✔	✔	✘	points

1 This sequence of dot patterns shows square numbers. Draw the next three patterns in the sequence.

1   4   9

The 8th number in the sequence is ⬭

2 Draw the next pattern of dots in this sequence.

4   6   8   10

The 8th number in the sequence is ⬭

3 Write the sequence of the first five numbers following the instructions.

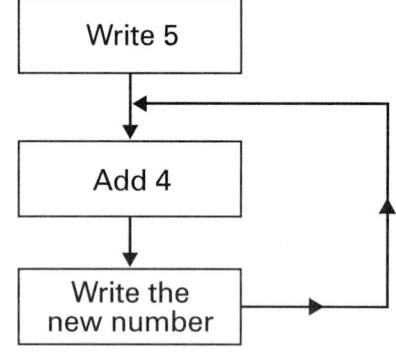

Write 5

Add 4

Write the
new number

▢ ▢ ▢ ▢ ▢

4 Underline the sequence which is formed using this rule:

| Start with 3, add 6 each time. |

3   9   15   21   27

or

3   9   14   18   21

5 Ring the prime numbers in this sequence.

11   16   21   26   31   36   41

Name   **Date**

Follow instructions to generate sequences

6 Write down the sequence of the first five numbers using this rule.

> Start with 2. Multiply by 2 and subtract 1.

7 Write the sequence of the first five equivalent fractions formed using this rule.

> Start with $\frac{2}{5}$. Multiply the numerator and the denominator by 3.

8 Write down the sequence of five numbers given by this BASIC program.

```
10    FOR NUMBER = 2 TO 6
20    PRINT NUMBER + 3
30    NEXT NUMBER
40    END
```

9 Write down the sequence of five numbers given by this BASIC program.

```
10    FOR NUMBER = 2 TO 6
20    PRINT NUMBER * NUMBER
30    NEXT NUMBER
40    END
```

The square root of 36 is

10 Write down the sequence of five numbers given by this BASIC program.

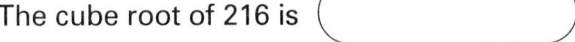

```
10    FOR NUMBER = 2 TO 6
20    PRINT NUMBER * NUMBER * NUMBER
30    NEXT NUMBER
40    END
```

The cube root of 216 is

11 Write down the next three equivalent fractions in this sequence.

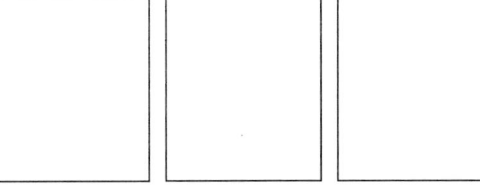

$$\frac{3}{4} \quad \frac{9}{12} \quad \frac{27}{36}$$

1 Write a formula for the cost (*c*) in pounds of three computer games at £*d* each.

2 A plank is *r* cm long. A man cut off *s* cm. Write a formula for the amount (*a*) he has left (in centimetres).

3 Two fences are *t* metres and *u* metres long. Together, their total length is 30 metres. Write a formula linking *t* and *u*.

4 Plants are arranged in *x* rows. The number of plants in each row is *y*. There are 24 plants altogether. Write a formula linking *x* and *y*.

5 Tom's age is *t* years. Mira is four years younger than Tom. Write a formula to express Mira's age (*m*) in years.

6 A group of *p* children are divided equally into *c* classes. How many children are there in each class?

7 I think of a number *x*, subtract 1, then multiply the answer by *x*. The result is *r*. Write a formula linking these facts.

8 Find the function linking these values of *a* and *b*.

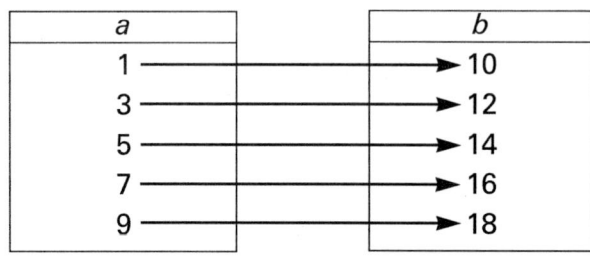

a	*b*
1	10
3	12
5	14
7	16
9	18

9 Write the functions linking the values of *x* and *y*.

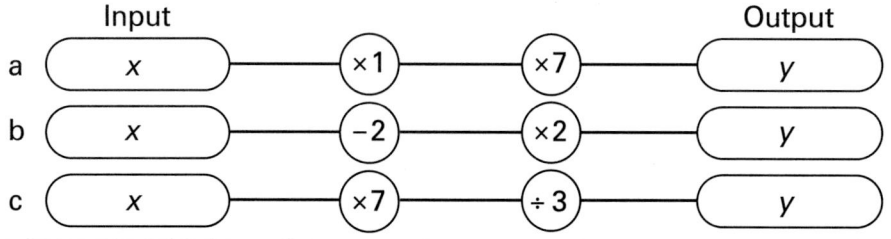

	Input			Output	Function
a	*x*	×1	×7	*y*	
b	*x*	−2	×2	*y*	
c	*x*	×7	÷3	*y*	

10 Write an equation to represent these amounts which balance.

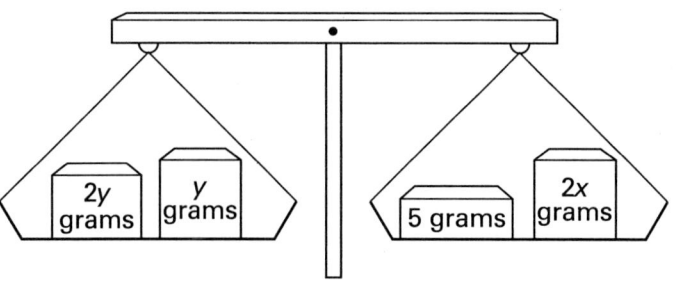

```
=
```

11 The perimeter (*p*) of a rectangle is given by the formula $p = 2(t + q)$.

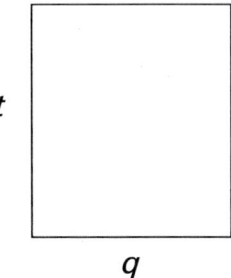

t

q

    a If *t* is 7 cm and *q* is 4 cm then *p* = ( )cm

    b If *p* is 36 cm and *t* is 10 cm then *q* = ( )cm

12 Write a formula for the
perimeter (*p*) of this shape.

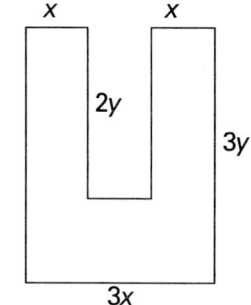

x   *x*

2*y*

3*y*

3*x*

13

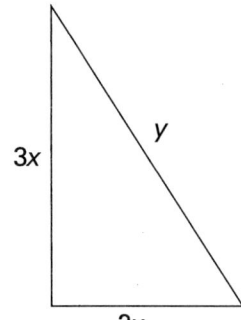

3*x*

y

2*x*

    a Write a formula for the perimeter (*p*) of this triangle.

    b What is the perimeter if *x* is 3 cm and *y* is 8 cm?

    cm

14 We can convert temperatures from degrees Fahrenheit (*F*) to degrees Celsius (*C*) using this
formula:

$$F = \frac{9}{5}C + 32$$

If the temperature is 11°C,
what is it in °F,
to the nearest degree?

°F

You need: ruler, protractor, compasses, scissors, sellotape

1 What is the length of this line, in millimetres?

_____

(   ) mm

2 Measure each angle to the nearest degree.

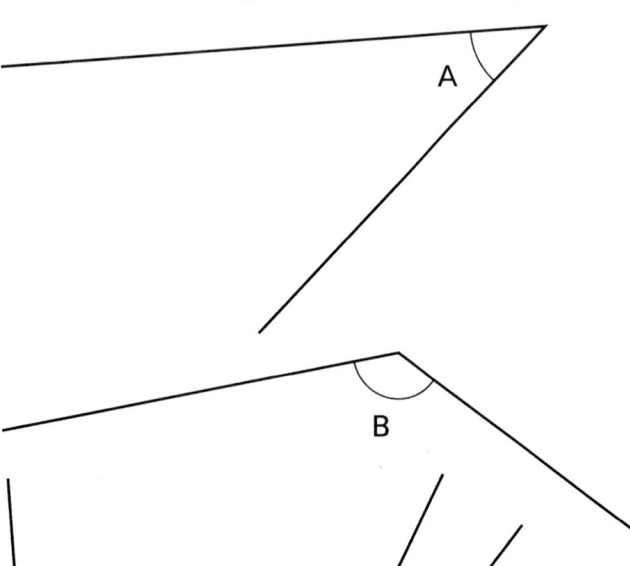

Angle A = (   )°

Angle B = (   )°

Angle C = (   )°

Angle D = (   )°

Angle E = (   )°

Angle F = (   )°

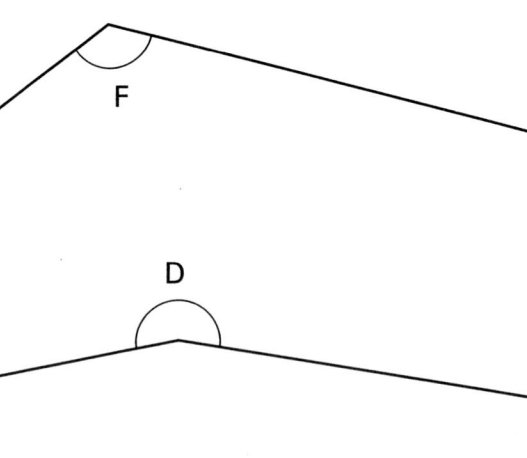

3 Measure the sides and angles of this triangle.

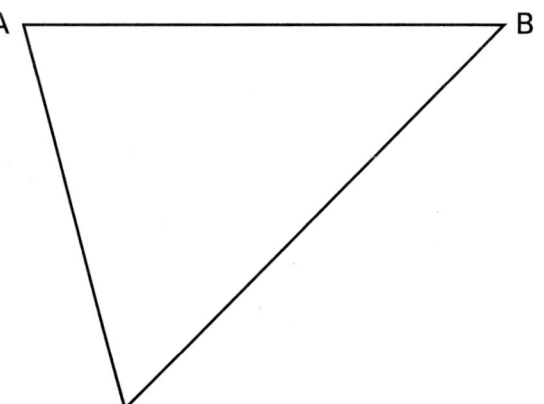

a Length AB is (   ) cm

b Length BC is (   ) cm

c Length AC is (   ) cm

d Angle CAB is (   )°

e Angle ABC is (   )°

f Angle BCA is (   )°

4 In the space, draw these angles.

    a A = 63°

    b B = 157°

    c C = 268°

Mark each angle with the letter, an arc and the number of degrees, e.g.

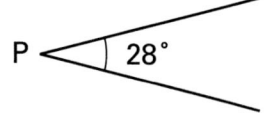

P   28°

5 Use this space to construct the triangle PQR in which

PQ is 5.7 cm
∠RPQ is 36°
∠PQR is 55°.

    a Length PR is (　　　　　) cm

    b Length QR is (　　　　　) cm

6 Use strong paper or card to construct a square-based pyramid. Use a net like this with the given lengths and angles.

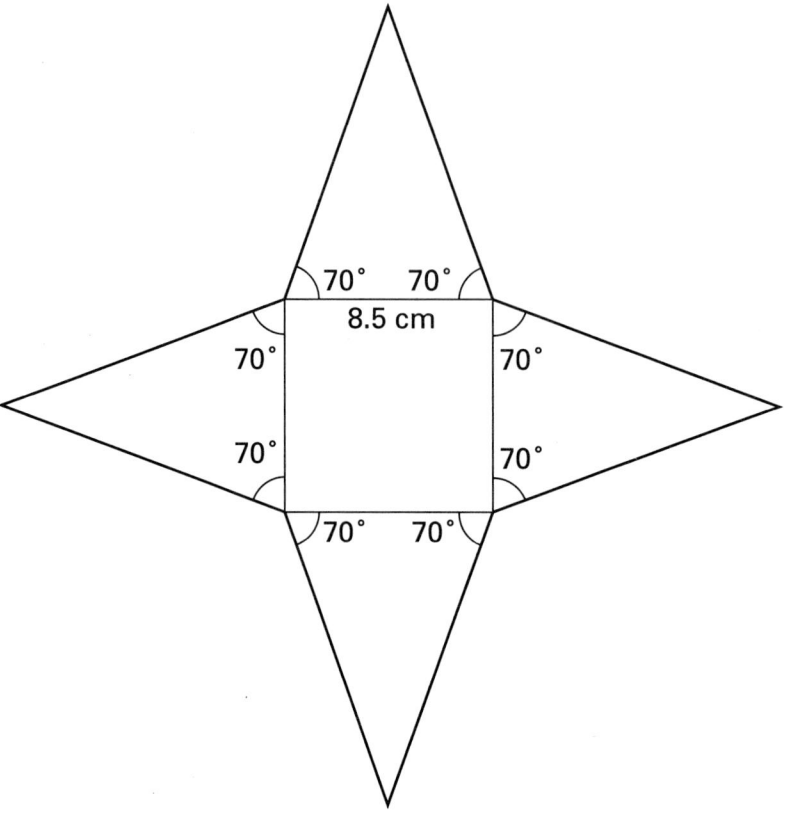

7 Use strong paper or card to construct a triangular prism like this, with the given lengths and angles.

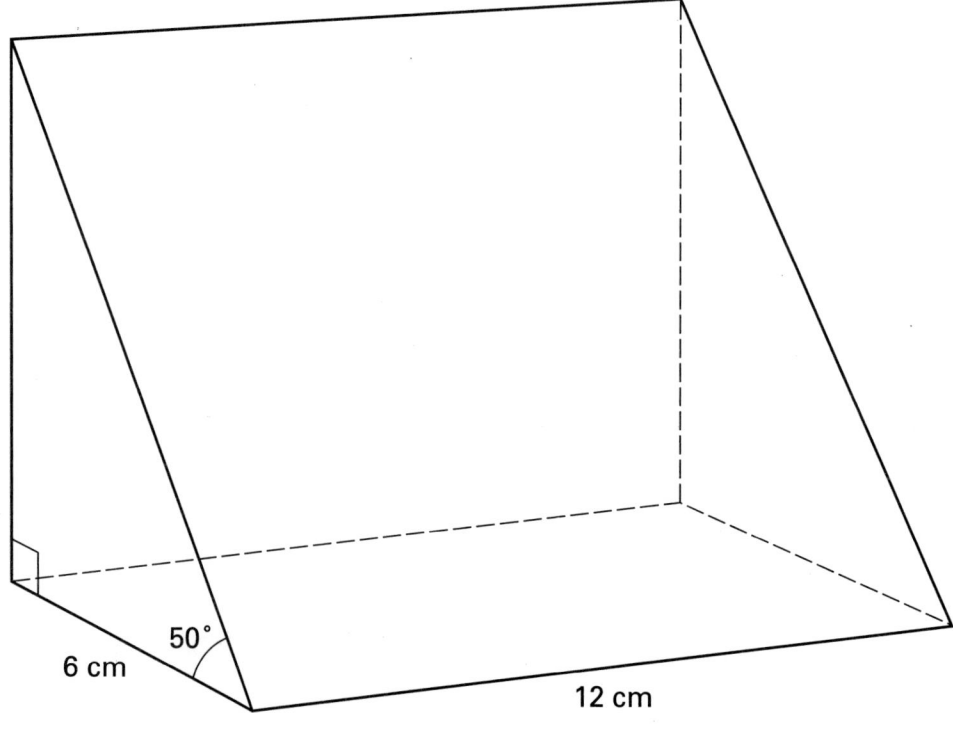

1 Write down the sizes of the three other angles in this diagram.

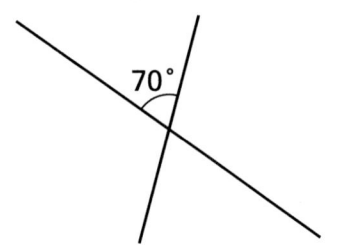

70°

2 Mark the angles that are equal to the angle marked with a star.

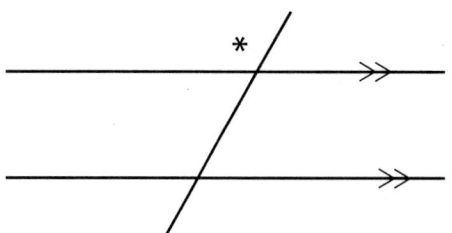

*

3 Two angles which add up to 180°

are ⬭

and ⬭ .

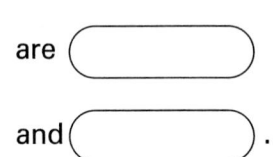

4

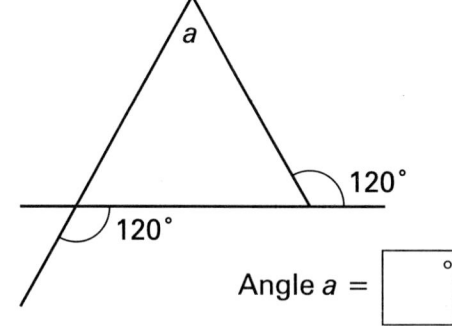

a

120°

120°

Angle *a* = ☐°

5

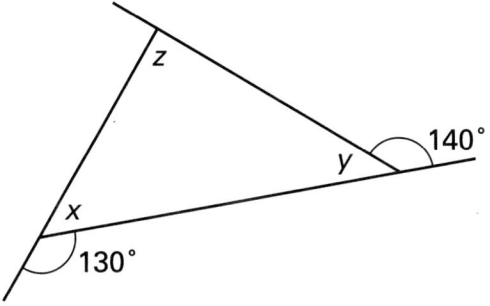

z

140°

y

x

130°

a Angle *x* = ⬭ °

b Angle *y* = ⬭ °

c Angle *z* = ⬭ °

6

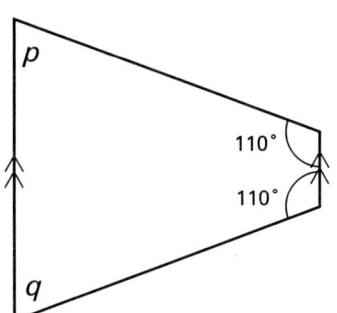

p

110°

110°

q

a Angle *p* = ⬭ °

b Angle *q* = ⬭ °

7

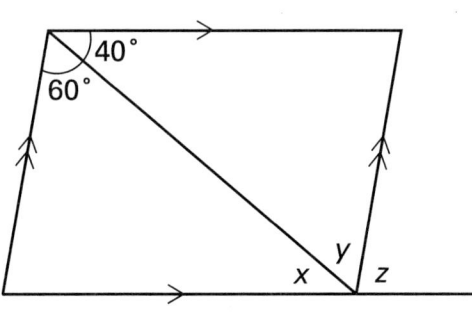

40°

60°

y

x *z*

a Angle *x* = ⬭ °

b Angle *y* = ⬭ °·

c Angle *z* = ⬭ °

8 Tick two adjacent angles.

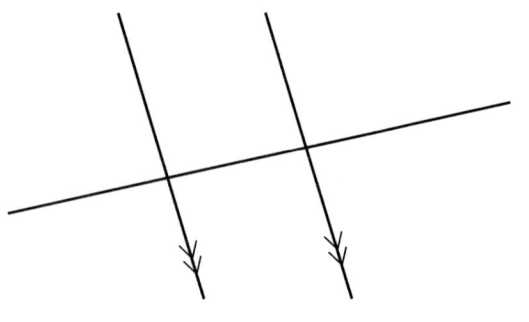

9 Tick two vertically opposite angles.

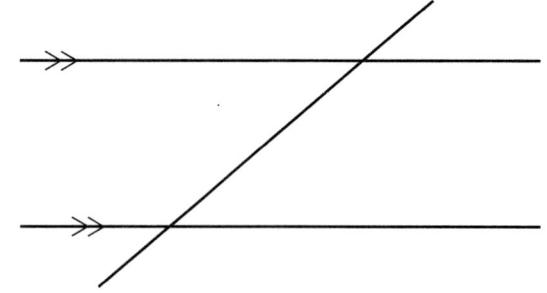

10 Tick two corresponding angles.

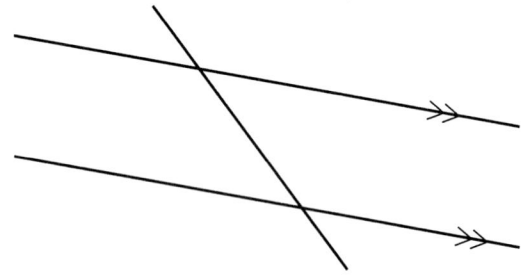

11 Tick two alternate angles.

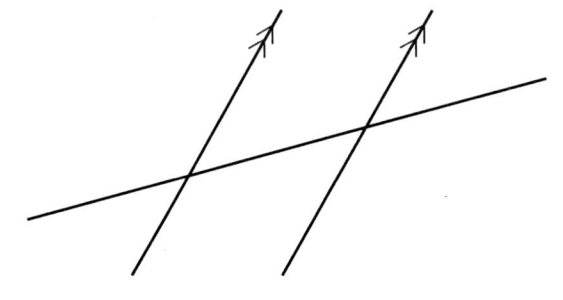

12

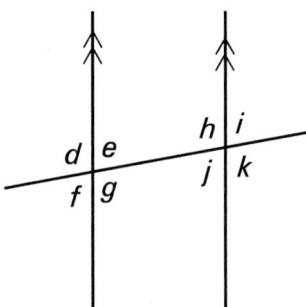

a Two adjacent angles are ( ) and ( ) .

b Two vertically opposite angles are ( ) and ( ) .

c Two corresponding angles are ( ) and ( ) .

d Two alternate angles are ( ) and ( ) .

13 Angle $x = ($ $)°$
in this rectangle.

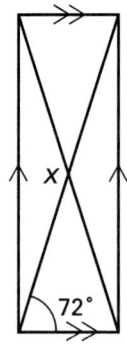

14 Angle $x = ($ $)°$

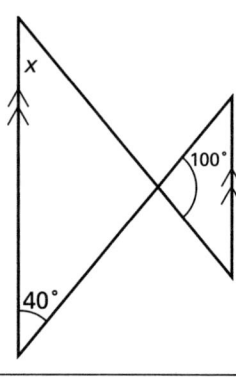

15 Angle $x = ($ $)°$

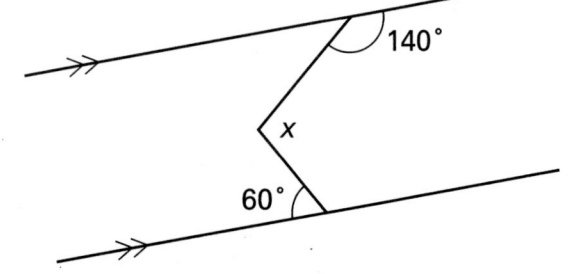

16 Angle $x = ($ $)°$

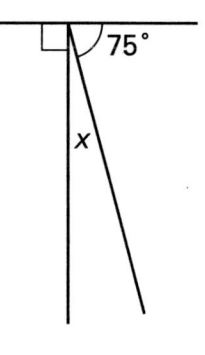

17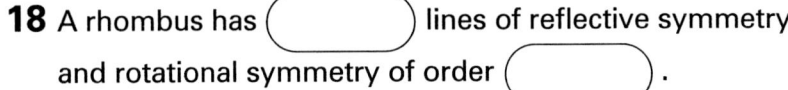

Which of these letters have

a reflective but not rotational symmetry

b rotational but not reflective symmetry

c reflective and rotational symmetry

d neither reflective nor rotational symmetry?

18 A rhombus has (   ) lines of reflective symmetry

and rotational symmetry of order (   ) .

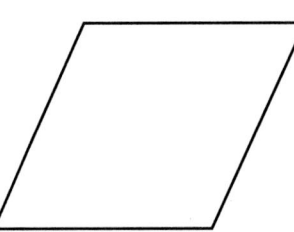

19 A rectangle has (   ) lines of reflective symmetry

and rotational symmetry of order (   ) .

20 Draw a shape with three lines of reflective symmetry.

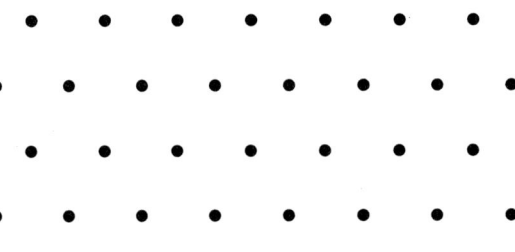

21 A triangular prism has [   ] planes of symmetry.

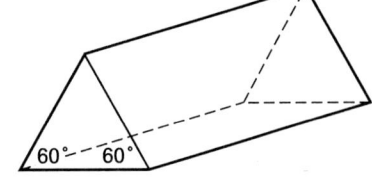

22 This 3-D shape has [   ] planes of symmetry.

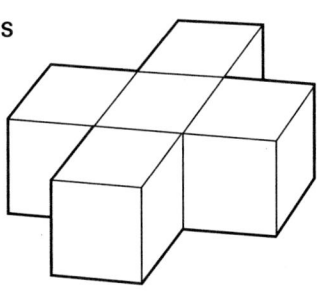

Mathscheck

Ma 4/5c

SERIES **II**

Name

Date

Use networks to solve problems

1 Travelling only across (→) or down (↓), how many different routes are there from X to Y?

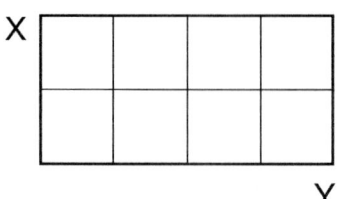

routes

2 This shape is traversable.

Show how on this dotted grid.

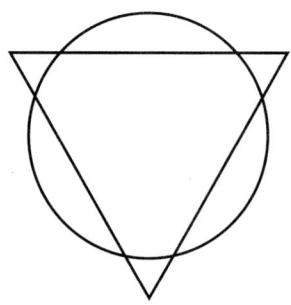

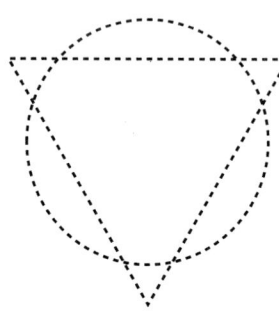

3 Six people met and they all shook hands with each other. Draw a network to show all the handshakes.

A
•

F •   • B

E •   • C

The total number of handshakes is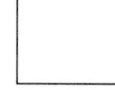

•
D

4 The postman's van starts and finishes at A. He visits each place only once and does not travel along the same road twice.

The **shortest** route he would take is A

A →

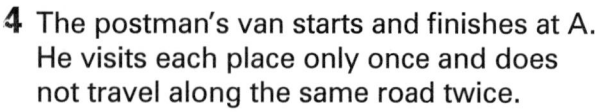

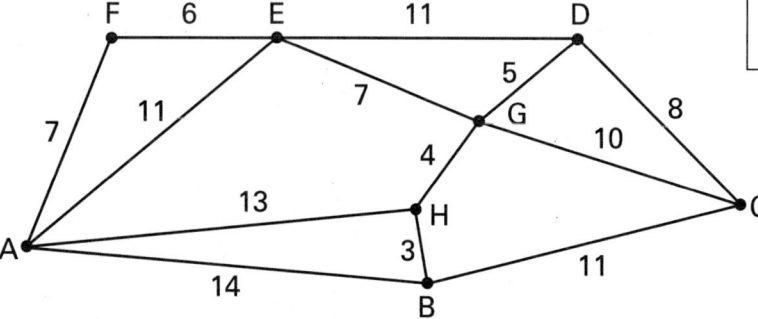

The length of the shortest route

is (   ) km

Mathscheck

Ma 4/5d
SERIES **II**

Name

Date

Find areas of plane shapes or volumes of simple solids

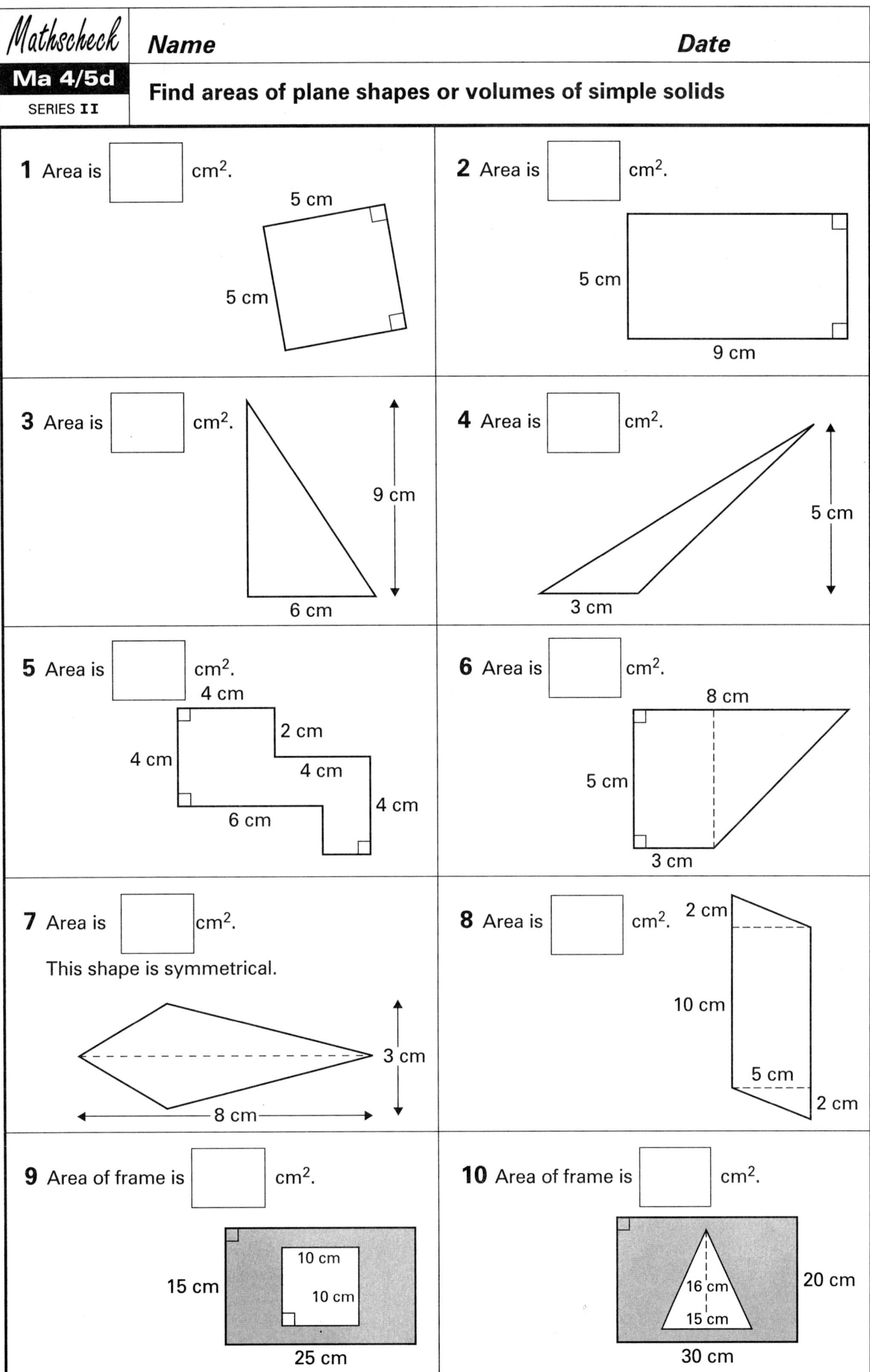

1 Area is ☐ cm².

5 cm

5 cm

2 Area is ☐ cm².

5 cm

9 cm

3 Area is ☐ cm².

9 cm

6 cm

4 Area is ☐ cm².

5 cm

3 cm

5 Area is ☐ cm².

4 cm

2 cm

4 cm

4 cm

6 cm

4 cm

6 Area is ☐ cm².

8 cm

5 cm

3 cm

7 Area is ☐ cm².

This shape is symmetrical.

3 cm

8 cm

8 Area is ☐ cm².

2 cm

10 cm

5 cm

2 cm

9 Area of frame is ☐ cm².

10 cm

10 cm

15 cm

25 cm

10 Area of frame is ☐ cm².

16 cm

15 cm

20 cm

30 cm

11 Volume is [ ] cm³.

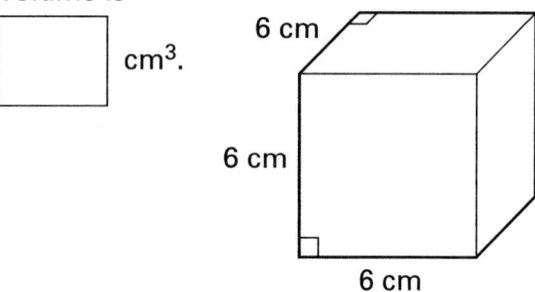

6 cm

6 cm

6 cm

12 Volume is [ ] cm³.

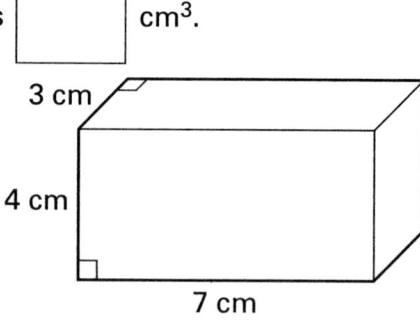

3 cm

4 cm

7 cm

13 Volume is [ ] cm³.

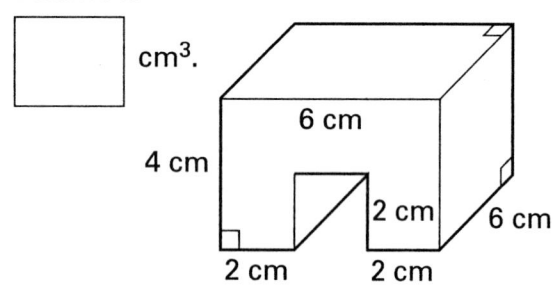

6 cm

4 cm

2 cm

6 cm

2 cm   2 cm

14 Volume is [ ] cm³.

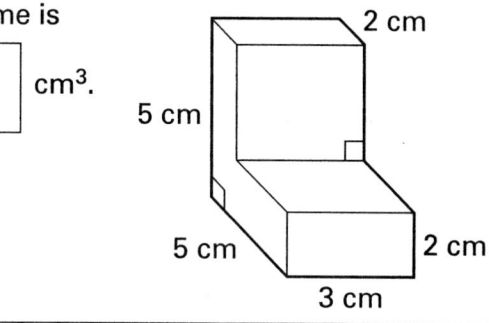

2 cm

5 cm

5 cm   2 cm

3 cm

15 Volume is [ ] cm³.

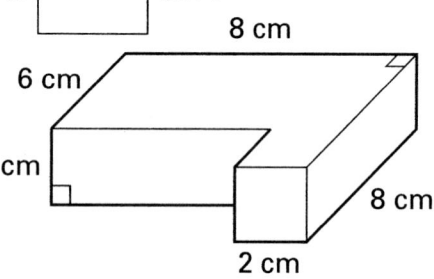

8 cm

6 cm

2 cm

8 cm

2 cm

16 Volume is [ ] cm³.

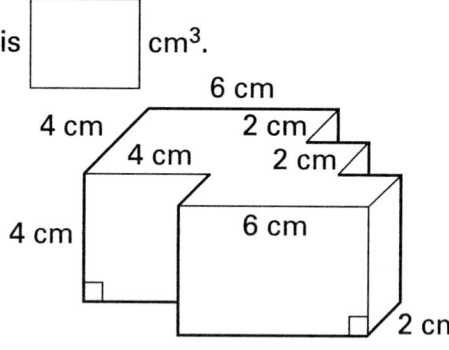

6 cm

4 cm   2 cm

4 cm   2 cm

4 cm   6 cm

2 cm

17 Volume is [ ] cm³.

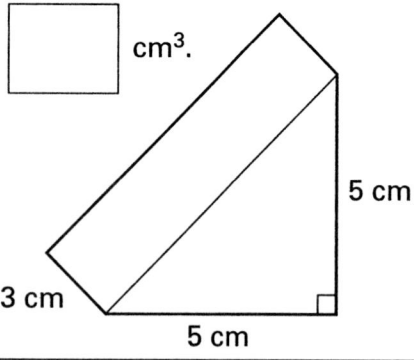

5 cm

3 cm

5 cm

18 Volume is [ ] cm³.

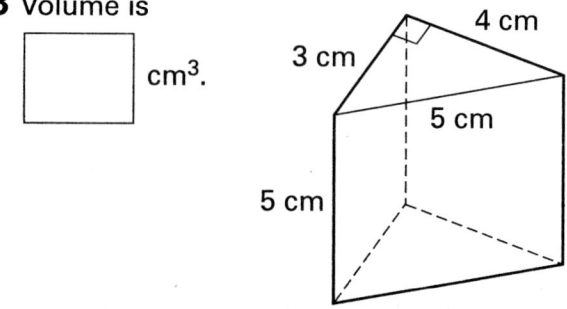

4 cm

3 cm

5 cm

5 cm

19 The total height of the shape is 11 cm.
The volume of the whole shape
is [ ] cm³.

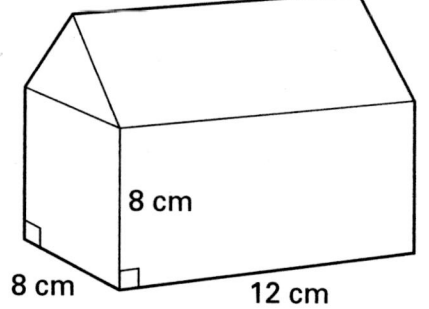

8 cm

8 cm   12 cm

Use a computer database to draw conclusions

Use a computer database package and have your work checked after each activity.

Tick when completed.

1 Set up a database file to hold 12 records, each containing 4 fields.

2 Enter this data about dinosaurs then save the file onto a floppy disc.

Record	Field 1	Field 2	Field 3	Field 4
	Name	Food	Habitat	Length in metres
1	Allosaurus	meat	land	11
2	Triceratops	plant	land, water	11
3	Iguanodon	plant	land	5
4	Polacanthus	plant	land	12
5	Pteranodon	fish	air	8
6	Pterodactylus	insect	air	2
7	Stegosaurus	plant	land	10
8	Diplodocus	plant	land, water	28
9	Plesiosaur	fish	water	12
10	Ichthyosaur	fish	water	12
11				
12				

3 Add this record to the database file and save it again.

Record	11	Fabrosaurus	plant	land	1

4 Sort the records into alphabetic order.

5 Sort the records into length order, smallest first.

6 Name the smallest plant-eating dinosaur.

7 Name the two longest dinosaurs which only live in water.

a

b

1 A weekend survey of the colours of 50 cars produced this data.

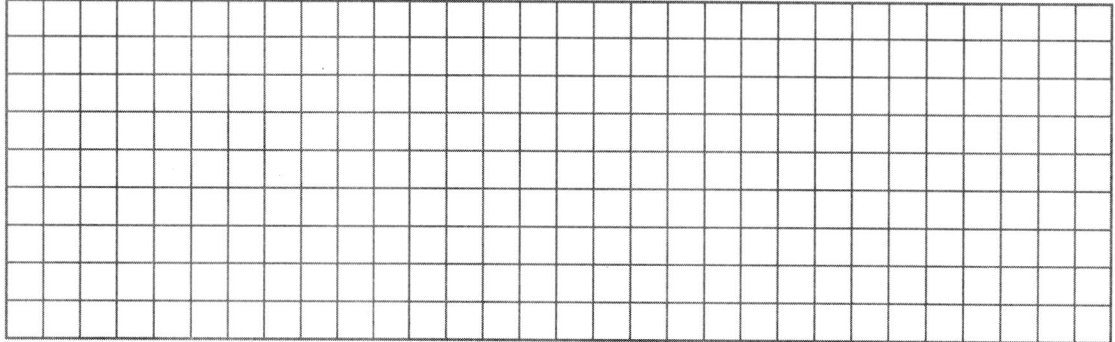

> grey   black   red   red   white   blue   brown   red   grey   green
> green   grey   green   black   brown   brown   blue   red   blue   red
> red   white   blue   brown   green   grey   blue   red   blue   grey
> red   white   red   blue   red   grey   green   blue   red   blue
> brown   green   grey   red   white   red   grey   blue   white   red

a Design and draw a recording sheet for collecting the data.

b Write down two pieces of information shown by the collected data.

2 Design an observation sheet on which to record data about the number of letters in each word on one page of an encyclopaedia.

a Use it to carry out the collection of data.

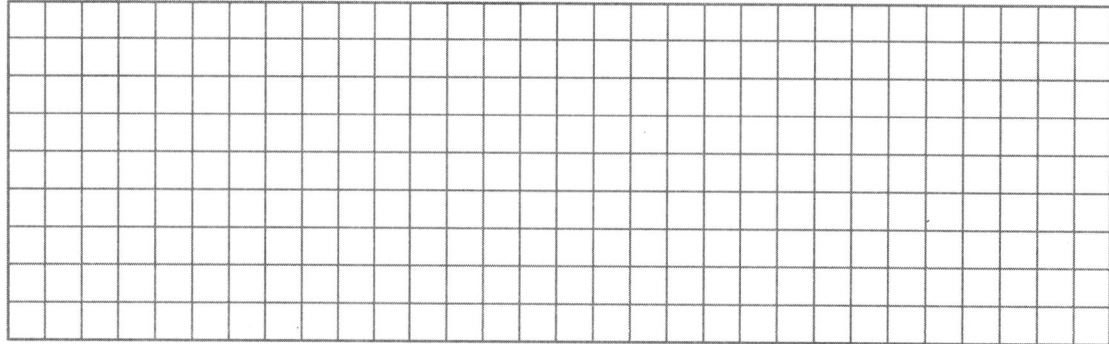

b Write down two pieces of information shown by the data.

3 This data shows the results of a 200 metre running event.
The times are in seconds.

30.0	31.2	31.6	30.0	31.4	30.8	31.2	30.0	30.2
29.6	30.0	31.6	30.8	31.6	30.8	29.4	31.6	31.2
29.4	31.8	32.6	31.0	32.0	30.4	31.8	33.2	32.0
30.2	31.2	32.0	31.8	31.0	31.4	30.4	31.0	32.0
31.4	30.4	31.6	31.8	30.6	31.2	30.8	29.8	32.4

   a   Draw and complete a frequency table of the results using five equal class intervals.

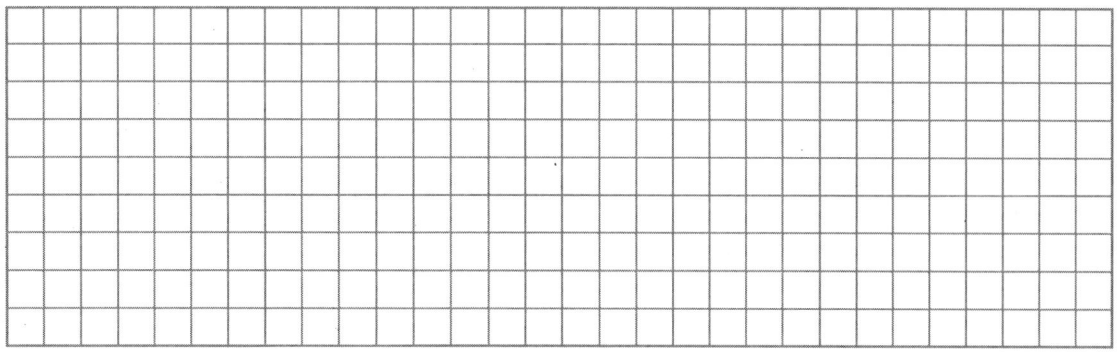

   b   Draw a graph of the results.

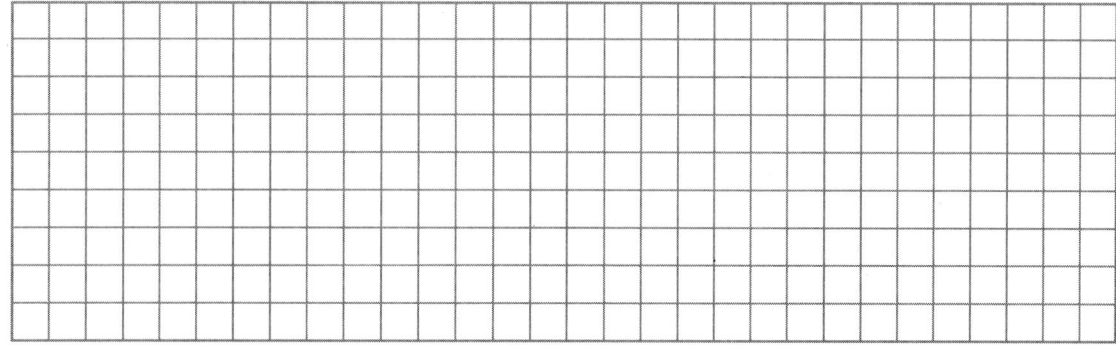

   c   Write down two pieces of information shown by the graph or frequency table.

1 In a survey, 36 people were asked to taste four drinks and say which they preferred. The results were:

apple juice   13
orange juice   7
lime juice   9
pineapple juice   7

Construct a pie chart from the data.

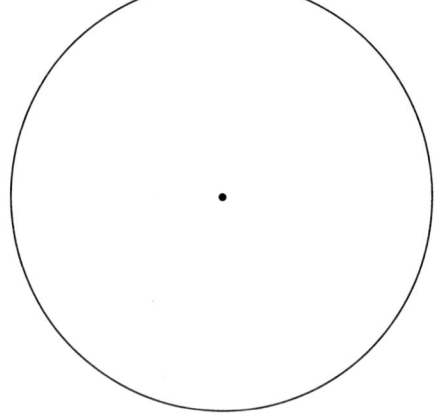

2 Construct a pie chart from the information shown in the bar chart.

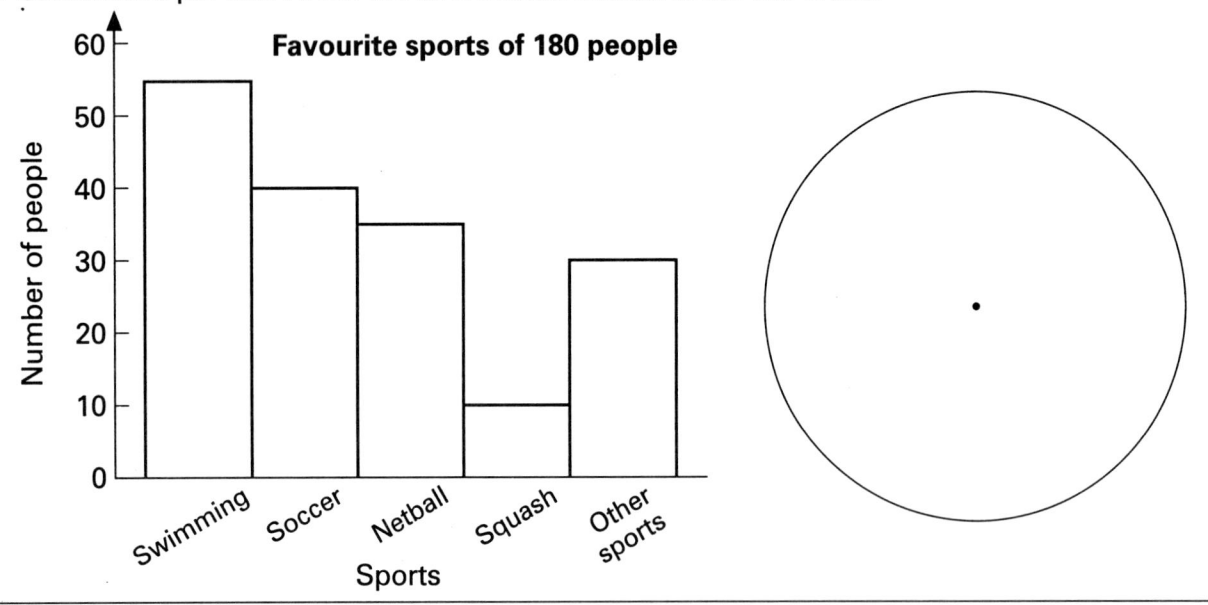

3 In a survey, 24 people were asked to name their favourite colour from a choice of four. This pie chart was drawn from the results.

a The angle for the red section is [   ]°.

b Write down the numbers of people who chose each colour.

red ⟶ [   ]

blue ⟶ [   ]

green ⟶ [   ]

yellow ⟶ [   ]

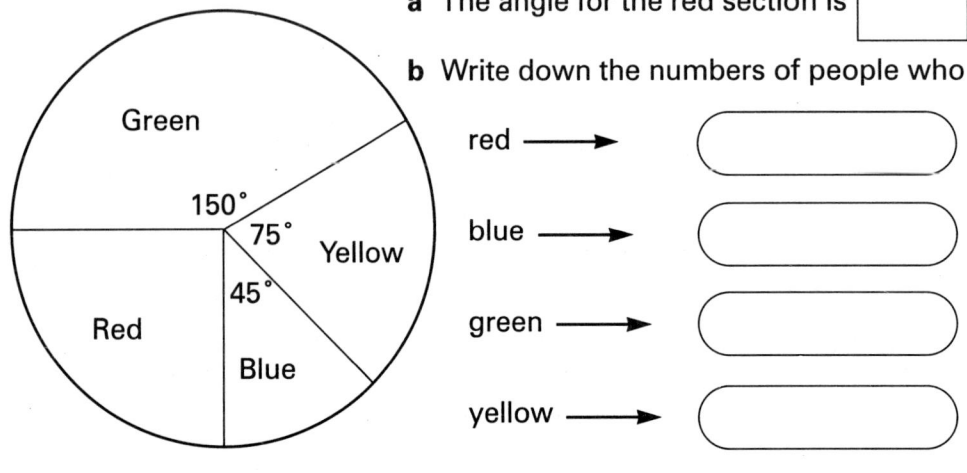

4 This is a graph showing the relation between centimetres and inches.

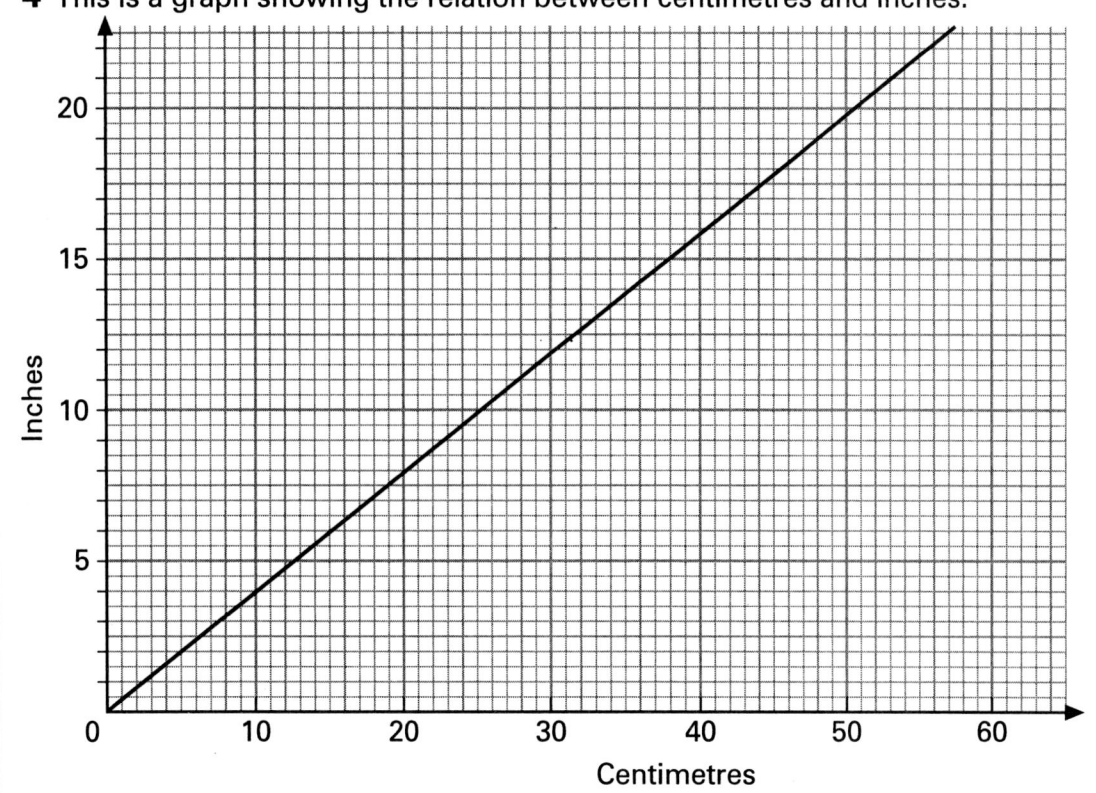

a 14 inches = ⬭ cm   **b** 18 cm = ⬭ inches

5 Draw a conversion graph to convert between ounces and grams.

1 ounce = 28.35 g and 100 g = 3.53 ounces

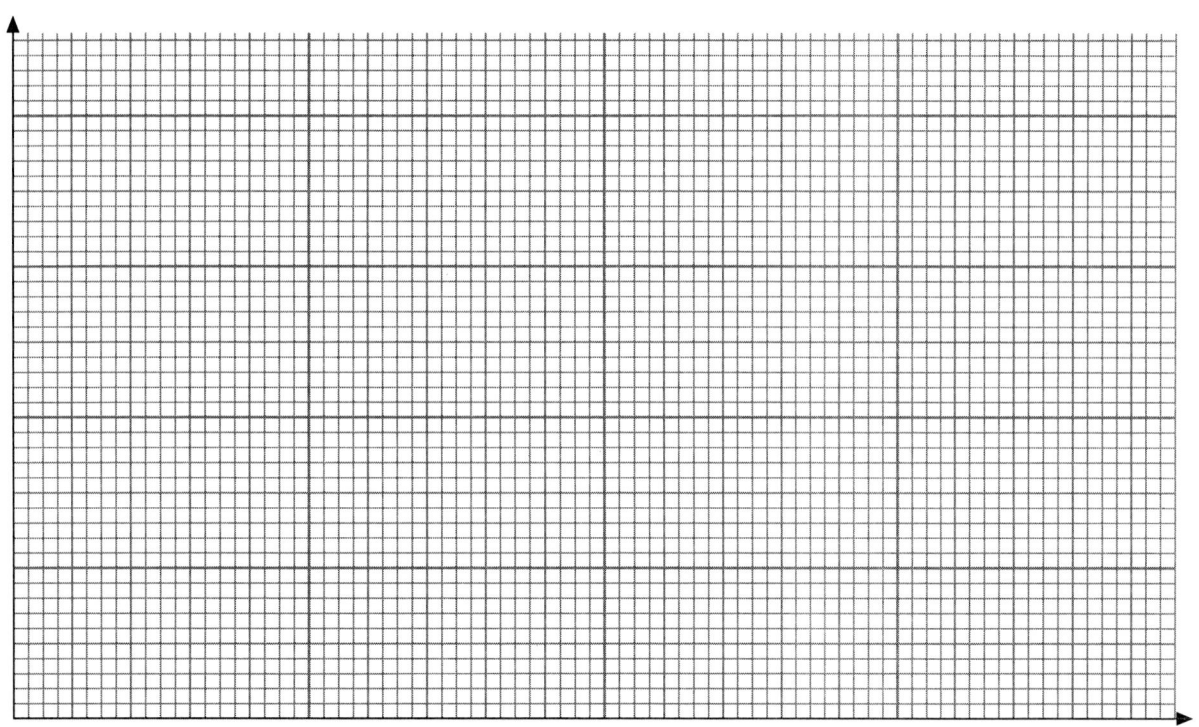

1 Write T for true or F for false in each box.

The spinner is spun 20 times.

a There will be **exactly** 10 whites and 10 greens.

b There will **never** be 20 greens in a row.

c There **might** be different numbers of whites and greens.

d There will **usually** be at least one green.

e There will **always** be some whites and some greens.

f There will **usually** be at least one white.

If the experiment is repeated 50 times to give 1000 results:

g There will **exactly** 500 whites and 500 greens.

h There will **never** be 100 greens in a row.

i There will be **usually** be some whites and some greens.

j It is **likely** that there will be **about** 500 whites and 500 greens.

2 Which of these situations would allow you to calculate an exact probability and which would have to be estimated?

Write 'exact' or 'estimate' in each box

a The probability that the next car to pass the school gate will be a Ford

b The probability of picking the three of clubs from a full pack of cards

c The probability that it will snow next Wednesday

d The probability of throwing an even number on a normal die

3 You can go to school on Monday, Tuesday, Wednesday, Thursday or Friday (5 days).
Write down two reasons why the probability of going to school on Monday might **not** be $\frac{1}{5}$.

a

b

4 There are four methods for estimating probabilities.

A Using the idea of equally likely outcomes	**B** By experiment	**C** By survey	**D** Using data collected earlier
Example: The probability of the spinner stopping on red is $\frac{1}{3}$.	Example: coloured beads in a bag. Keep drawing out a bead, recording the result and replacing the bead.	Example: collecting and recording data from observation or by questioning people	Example: look at data kept in such places as schools, hospitals, companies or government offices

Choose the best method (A, B, C or D) for estimating the probability that:

a the next car you see will be blue

b the tide in London will be high next Monday

c a single throw of a die will score an odd number

d if you drop ten cups, two will break

e the toss of a coin will produce a 'tail'.

Answers for Level 5

The answers for Series I and Series II papers are given together
for each Statement of Attainment

Mathscheck — Name — Date

Ma 2/5a
SERIES I

Use an appropriate non-calculator method to multiply or divide two numbers

1 Calculate (showing your working):

472 × 24

11 328

2 Calculate (showing your working):

217 × 93

20 181

3 Calculate (showing your working):

345 ÷ 23

15

4 Calculate (showing your working):

592 ÷ 16

37

5 A group of 326 people each paid £17 to go on a camping trip. How much money was paid altogether? (Show your working.)

£5542

6 A sum of £285 was shared equally among 15 classes to spend on library books. How much did each class receive? (Show your working.)

£19

Mathscheck — Name — Date

Ma 2/5a
SERIES II

Use an appropriate non-calculator method to multiply or divide two numbers

1 Calculate (showing your working):

329 × 32

10 528

2 Calculate (showing your working):

176 × 87

15 312

3 Calculate (showing your working):

364 ÷ 28

13

4 Calculate (showing your working):

782 ÷ 17

46

5 A shop sold 278 games discs for £13 each. How much money was paid altogether? (Show your working.)

£3614

6 A prize of £506 was shared equally among 22 friends. How much did each person receive? (Show your working.)

£23

Mathscheck

Ma 2/5a SERIES II — Use an appropriate non-calculator method to multiply or divide two numbers

7 A crate holds 24 bottles. How many crates would be needed to carry 332 bottles? (Show your working.)

14 crates

8 Calculate the cost in pounds and pence of buying 175 burgers for a school party if each burger costs 57p. (Show your working.)

£99.75

9 Work these out in your head. Write down the answers.

a $30 \times 60 =$ 1800
b $300 \times 20 =$ 6000
c $40 \times 80 =$ 3200
d $400 \times 70 =$ 28 000

10 Work these out in your head. Write down the answers.

a $600 \div 30 =$ 20
b $4000 \div 50 =$ 80
c $8000 \div 400 =$ 20
d $8000 \div 20 =$ 400

11 Write the correct numbers in the empty boxes.

a 40 → $\times 300$ → 12 000 → $\div 60$ → 200
b 250 → $\times 40$ → 10 000 → $\div 50$ → 200
c 100 → $\times 5$ → 500 → $\div 20$ → 25

Mathscheck

Ma 2/5a SERIES I — Use an appropriate non-calculator method to multiply or divide two numbers

7 Calculate how many buses are needed to take 223 people on a trip, if each bus holds 47 people. (Show your working.)

5 buses

8 Calculate the cost in pounds and pence of buying 295 cans of Cola for a school party if each can costs 33p. (Show your working.)

£97.35

9 Work these out in your head. Write down the answers.

a $50 \times 20 =$ 1000
b $200 \times 30 =$ 6000
c $30 \times 70 =$ 2100
d $300 \times 90 =$ 27 000

10 Work these out in your head. Write down the answers.

a $400 \div 20 =$ 20
b $6000 \div 20 =$ 300
c $8000 \div 200 =$ 40
d $8000 \div 40 =$ 200

11 Write the correct numbers in the empty boxes.

a 50 → $\times 200$ → 10 000 → $\div 40$ → 250
b 40 → $\times 50$ → 2000 → $\div 20$ → 100
c 200 → $\times 5$ → 1000 → $\div 20$ → 50

Left sheet (Series I)

Mathscheck | **Name** | | **Date**

Ma 2/5b
SERIES I

Find fractions or percentages of quantities

1

a What fraction of the squares contains stars? (Write it in its lowest terms.)

$$\frac{7}{20}$$

b What percentage of the squares is empty?

65 %

c What percentage of the squares contains stars?

35 %

2 Calculate $\frac{2}{5}$ of 800 grams.

320 g

3 Calculate 45% of 40 kg.

18 kg

4 Write $2\frac{1}{2}$% as a fraction in its lowest terms.

$\frac{1}{40}$

5 What is 100% of £1?

£ 1

6 Calculate $\frac{5}{8}$ of £176.

£ 110

7 Calculate 22% of £99.

£ 21.78

Right sheet (Series II)

Mathscheck | **Name** | | **Date**

Ma 2/5b
SERIES II

Find fractions or percentages of quantities

1

a What fraction of the squares contain dots? (Write it in its lowest terms.)

$$\frac{9}{20}$$

b What percentage of the squares are empty?

55 %

c What percentage of the squares contain dots?

45 %

2 Calculate $\frac{3}{5}$ of £700.

£ 420

3 Calculate 65% of 80 metres.

52 m

4 Write $12\frac{1}{2}$% as a fraction in its lowest terms.

$\frac{1}{8}$

5 What is 100% of 11 km?

11 km

6 Calculate $\frac{3}{8}$ of 2000 g.

750 g

7 Calculate 37% of £84.

£ 31.08

Ma 2/5b — SERIES I

Find fractions or percentages of quantities

8 In a class of 35 pupils, two-fifths are boys.

a How many boys are there? `14`

b How many girls are there? `21`

9 What is 90p as a percentage of £2.40? `37.5` %

10 A woman gave an amount of money to local charities. She gave:
20% of the money to the hospital
50% of the money to a playgroup
and £30 to an animal welfare group.
How much money did she give away altogether?

£ `100`

11 In June, it rained on 12 days.

a What fraction of the whole month was rainy? `$\frac{12}{30}$ or $\frac{6}{15}$ or $\frac{2}{5}$`

b What percentage of the whole month was dry? `60` %

12 Look at these offers and tick the one that is the best value.

☐ Cassettes: £2 off if you spend £8
☐ Chocolate: 19p off a 70p bar
☑ Books: £3 off if you spend £10

Ma 2/5b — SERIES II

Find fractions or percentages of quantities

8 On a shelf of 75 books, three-fifths are fiction.

a How many fiction books are there? `45`

b How many non-fiction books are there? `30`

9 What is 75p as a percentage of £2.50? `30` %

10 A man gave an amount of money to local charities. He gave:
15% of the money to the Old Folks' Home
60% of the money to a Youth Club
and £50 to a local Cats' Home.
How much money did he give away altogether?

£ `200`

11 In September, it was sunny on 18 days.

a What fraction of the whole month was sunny? `$\frac{18}{30}$ or $\frac{9}{15}$ or $\frac{3}{5}$`

b What percentage of the whole month was not sunny? `40` %

12 Look at these offers and tick the one that is the best value.

☑ Trainers: £3 off every £12 you spend
☐ Shorts: £1 off every £5 you spend
☐ Shirts: 22% off everything

71

Ma 2/5c
SERIES I

Refine estimations by 'trial and improvement' methods

1 Write these numbers correct to 1 decimal place.

a 6.371 → 6.4

b 2.946 → 3.0

c 0.882 → 0.9

2 Write these numbers correct to 3 decimal places.

a 3.26571 → 3.266

b 8.55555 → 8.556

c 0.002631 → 0.003

3 Write these numbers correct to 1 significant figure.

a 3758 → 4000

b 39.23 → 40

c 0.026 → 0.03

4 Write these numbers correct to 3 significant figures.

a 3293.15 → 3290

b 3.027 → 3.03

c 0.00123 → 0.00123

5 a Use a trial and improvement method to find the amount each person would get if £500 were shared equally among three people.

b The amount correct to 3 significant figures is £167

6 a Use a trial and improvement method to find the length of one side of a small square table if the area is 2000 cm².

b The length of the side, correct to 3 decimal places, is 44.721 cm

---

Ma 2/5c
SERIES II

Refine estimations by 'trial and improvement' methods

1 Write these numbers correct to 1 decimal place.

a 3.542 → 3.5

b 12.295 → 12.3

c 6.028 → 6.0

2 Write these numbers correct to 3 decimal places.

a 2.91678 → 2.917

b 4.54545 → 4.545

c 0.00561 → 0.006

3 Write these numbers correct to 1 significant figure.

a 2089 → 2000

b 32.85 → 30

c 0.0336 → 0.03

4 Write these numbers correct to 3 significant figures.

a 2119.83 → 2120

b 3.926 → 3.93

c 0.00882 → 0.00882

5 a Use a trial and improvement method to find the amount each person would get if £600 were shared equally among seven people.

b The amount correct to 3 significant figures is £85.70

6 a Use a trial and improvement method to find the length of one side of a small square table if the area is 3000 cm².

b The length of the side, correct to 3 decimal places, is 54.772 cm

Ma 2/5d SERIES II
Use units in context

1 Complete these.

a 1 litre = 1000 ml
b 100 cm = 1 m
c 1 cm = 10 mm
d 1 km = 1000 m
e 1 kg = 1000 g
f 1 tonne = 1000 kilograms
g 1000 m = 1 kilometre

2 Complete these.

a 33 cm = 330 mm
b 300 cm = 3 m
c 2.9 km = 2900 m
d 0.381 m = 38.1 cm
e 2222 m = 2.222 km
f 1234 mm = 1.234 m
g 0.8 cm = 8 mm

3 Complete these.

a 19.2 kg = 19 200 g
b 8.7 kg = 8 kg and 700 g
c 1637 g = 1.637 kg
d 1.9 tonnes = 1900 kg
e 0.33 kg = 330 g
f 2.7 litres = 2700 ml
g 0.01 litres = 10 ml

4 Add 400 ml and 0.85 litres. Give the answer in litres. = 1.25 litres

5 Add 0.72 metres and 280 cm. Give the answer in metres. = 3.52 m

6 From 1.3 metres subtract 53 cm. Give the answer in metres. = 0.77 metres

7 From 1 kg subtract 5 g. Give the answer in kilograms. = 0.995 kg

---

Ma 2/5d SERIES I
Use units in context

1 Complete these.

a 10 mm = 1 cm
b 1 m = 100 cm
c 1 km = 1000 m
d 1 m = 1000 mm
e 1000 g = 1 kg
f 1000 kg = 1 tonne
g 1000 ml = 1 litre

2 Complete these.

a 32.9 kg = 32 900 g
b 16.5 kg = 16 kg and 500 g
c 2184 g = 2.184 kg
d 2.4 tonnes = 2400 kg
e 0.45 kg = 450 g
f 1.5 litres = 1500 ml
g 0.023 litres = 23 ml

3 Complete these.

a 6.3 km = 6300 m
b 7842 m = 7.842 km
c 0.225 m = 22.5 cm
d 500 cm = 5 m
e 6233 mm = 6.233 m
f 54 cm = 540 mm
g 0.4 cm = 4 mm

4 Add 250 cm and 2.8 metres. Give the answer in metres. = 5.3 m

5 Add 2 kg 120 g and 0.5 kg. Give the answer in kilograms. = 2.62 kg

6 From 2.2 litres subtract 1500 ml. Give the answer in litres. = 0.7 litres

7 From 0.9 metres subtract 350 mm. Give the answer in millimetres. = 550 mm

Ma 2/5d — SERIES II
Use units in context

8 Complete these.

a 1 foot = **12** inches
b 1 yard = **3** feet
c 1 mile = **1760** yards
d 1 pound = **16** ounces
e 1 stone = **14** pounds
f 1 gallon = **8** pints

9 Ring the correct answer to each of these.

				ringed
a 1 inch is about	1 cm	2 cm	3 cm	**2·5 cm**
b 1 foot is about	20 cm	25 cm	35 cm	**30 cm**
c 1 yard is about	70 cm	80 cm	100 cm	**90 cm**
d 1 mile is about	5 km	3 km	1 km	**1·5 km**
e 1 ounce is about	50 g	40 g	10 g	**30 g**
f 1 pound is about	1 kg	$\frac{3}{4}$ kg	$\frac{1}{4}$ kg	**$\frac{1}{2}$ kg**
g 1 stone is about	14 kg	4 kg	6 kg	**2 kg**
h 1 pint is about	1 litre	800 ml	400 ml	**600 ml**
i 1 gallon is about	4 litres	$4\frac{1}{2}$ litres	5 litres	**$5\frac{1}{2}$ litres**

10

20°C 15°C 10°C 5°C 0°C −5°C −10°C −15°C −20°C

a Write these temperatures in order, highest first.

0°C   3°C   −7°C   −10°C   10°C

highest **10°C   3°C   0°C   −7°C   −10°C** lowest

b Complete this chart.

starting temperature	change in temperature	finishing temperature
2°C	falls 4°C	−2°C
10°C	falls 8°C	2°C
−9°C	rises 8°C	−1°C
−3°C	falls 7°C	−10°C
−6°C	rises 16°C	10°C

11 In a quiz you start with 8 points.
You add 3 points for a correct answer. ✔
You subtract 2 points for a wrong answer. ✗

How many points do these people end up with?

Name	1	2	3	4	5	6	7	8	9	10	Score
Eric	✗	✗	✗	✔	✔	✗	✔	✗	✔	✗	**8** points
Al	✔	✔	✗	✔	✗	✗	✗	✔	✔	✗	**8** points
Ella	✗	✔	✗	✗	✗	✗	✗	✔	✗	✗	**3** points
Aziz	✔	✔	✗	✗	✔	✔	✔	✔	✔	✗	**8** points
Mo	✗	✗	✗	✗	✗	✔	✔	✔	✔	✗	**13** points

Ma 2/5d — SERIES I
Use units in context

8 Complete these.

a 12 inches = **1** foot
b **3** feet = 1 yard
c 1760 yards = **1** mile
d **16** ounces = 1 pound
e 14 pounds = **1** stone
f **8** pints = 1 gallon

9 Ring the correct answer to each of these.

				ringed
a 1 inch is about	1 cm	2 cm	2 mm	**$2\frac{1}{2}$ cm**
b 1 foot is about	10 cm	20 cm	**30 cm**	12 cm
c 1 yard is about	**90 cm**	70 cm	100 cm	36 cm
d 1 mile is about	1 km	3 km	5 km	**$1\frac{1}{2}$ km**
e 1 ounce is about	10 g	40 g	20 g	**30 g**
f 1 pound is about	1 kg	$\frac{3}{4}$ kg	$\frac{1}{4}$ kg	**$\frac{1}{2}$ kg**
g 1 stone is about	4 kg	14 kg	**6 kg**	5 kg
h 1 pint is about	400 ml	800 ml	**600 ml**	700 ml
i 1 gallon is about	$2\frac{1}{2}$ litres	$4\frac{1}{2}$ litres	$3\frac{1}{2}$ litres	—

10

20°C 15°C 10°C 5°C 0°C −5°C −10°C −15°C −20°C

a Write these temperatures in order, highest first.

10°C   −15°C   6°C   0°C   −10°C

highest **10°C   6°C   0°C   −10°C   −15°C** lowest

b Complete this chart.

starting temperature	change in temperature	finishing temperature
10°C	falls 3°C	7°C
3°C	falls 5°C	−2°C
−7°C	rises 3°C	−4°C
−6°C	falls 4°C	−10°C
−2°C	rises 8°C	6°C

11 In a quiz you start with 8 points.
You add 2 points for a correct answer. ✔
You subtract 1 point for a wrong answer. ✗

How many points do these people end up with?

Name	1	2	3	4	5	6	7	8	9	10	Score
Jane	✔	✔	✗	✗	✗	✗	✔	✗	✗	✔	**7** points
Tom	✗	✗	✗	✔	✔	✔	✔	✔	✔	✗	**13** points
Sonia	✔	✗	✔	✗	✗	✗	✔	✔	✗	✗	**7** points
Kim	✗	✔	✗	✔	✔	✔	✗	✗	✔	✗	**10** points
Ali	✗	✗	✔	✔	✔	✔	✗	✗	✔	✗	**13** points

Ma 3/5a — SERIES I

Follow instructions to generate sequences

1 This sequence of dot patterns shows triangular numbers. Draw the next three patterns in the sequence.

1 3 6   10   15   21

The 8th number in the sequence is (36)

2 Draw the next pattern of dots in this sequence.

4 9 14   19

The 8th number in the sequence is (39)

3 Write the sequence of the first five numbers following the instructions.

Write 3 → Add 6 → Write the new number

[3] [9] [15] [21] [27]

4 Underline the sequence which is formed using this rule:

Start with 5, add 4 each time.

5   9   15   21   27

or

5   9   14   20   27

or

5   9   13   17   21

5 Ring the prime numbers in this sequence.

9   (13)   (17)   25   (29)   33

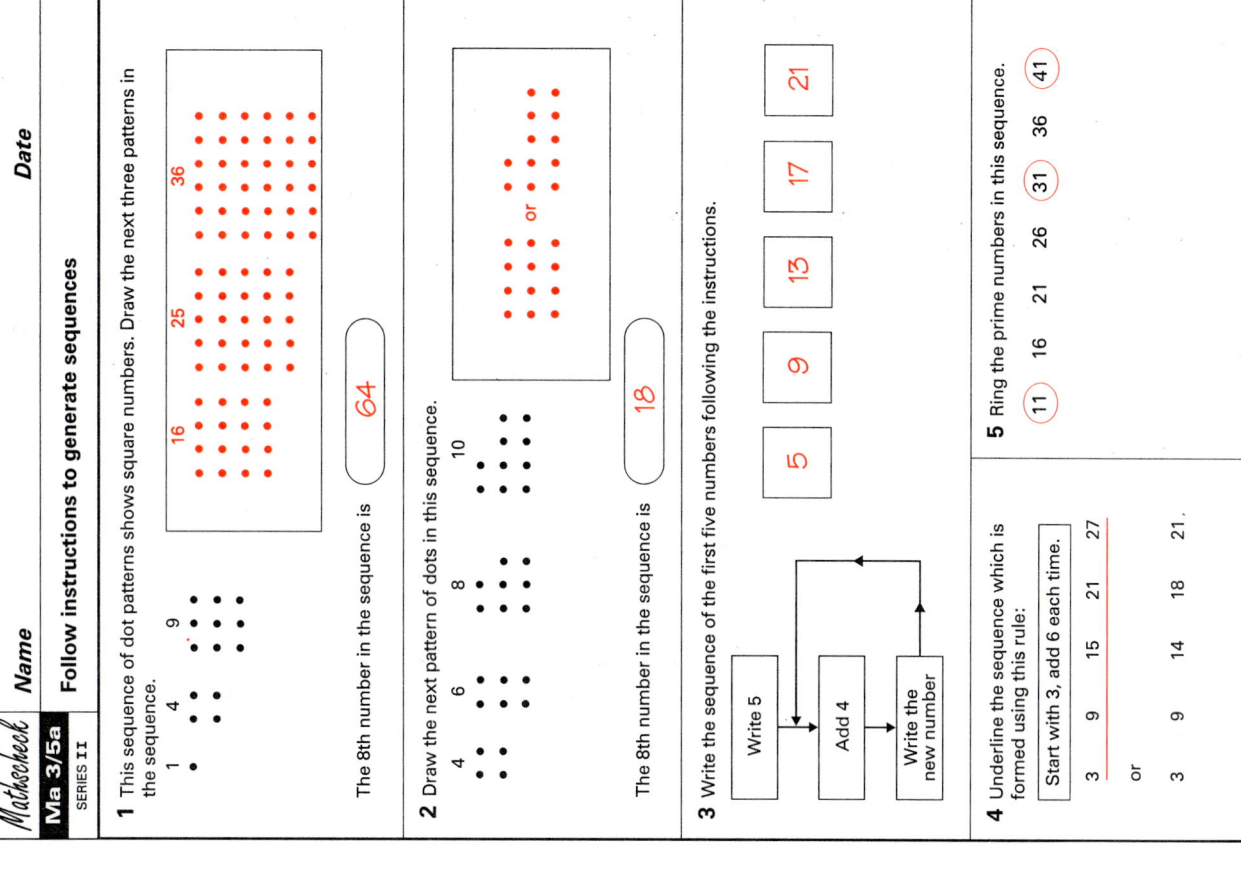

Ma 3/5a — SERIES II

Follow instructions to generate sequences

1 This sequence of dot patterns shows square numbers. Draw the next three patterns in the sequence.

1 4 9   16   25   36

The 8th number in the sequence is (64)

2 Draw the next pattern of dots in this sequence.

4 6 8   10

The 8th number in the sequence is (18)

3 Write the sequence of the first five numbers following the instructions.

Write 5 → Add 4 → Write the new number

[5] [9] [13] [17] [21]

4 Underline the sequence which is formed using this rule:

Start with 3, add 6 each time.

3   9   15   21   27

or

3   9   14   18   21

5 Ring the prime numbers in this sequence.

(11)   16   21   26   (31)   36   (41)

Ma 3/5a — SERIES I
Follow instructions to generate sequences

6 Write down the sequence of the first five numbers using this rule.

Start with 4. Multiply by 2 and add 1.

| 4 | 9 | 19 | 39 | 79 |

7 Write the sequence of the first five equivalent fractions formed using this rule.

Start with $\frac{2}{3}$. Multiply the numerator and the denominator by 2.

$\frac{2}{3}$ · $\frac{4}{6}$ · $\frac{8}{12}$ · $\frac{16}{24}$ · $\frac{32}{48}$

8 Write down the sequence of five numbers given by this BASIC program.

```
10  FOR NUMBER = 1 TO 5
20  PRINT NUMBER + 2
30  NEXT NUMBER
40  END
```

| 3 | 4 | 5 | 6 | 7 |

9 Write down the sequence of five numbers given by this BASIC program.

```
10  FOR NUMBER = 1 TO 5
20  PRINT NUMBER * NUMBER
30  NEXT NUMBER
40  END
```

| 1 | 4 | 9 | 16 | 25 |

The square root of 25 is 5

10 Write down the sequence of five numbers given by this BASIC program.

```
10  FOR NUMBER = 1 TO 5
20  PRINT NUMBER * NUMBER * NUMBER
30  NEXT NUMBER
40  END
```

| 1 | 8 | 27 | 64 | 125 |

The cube root of 125 is 5

11 Write down the next three equivalent fractions in this sequence.

$\frac{2}{5}$ · $\frac{6}{15}$ · $\frac{18}{45}$ · $\frac{54}{135}$ · $\frac{162}{405}$ · $\frac{486}{1215}$

Ma 3/5a — SERIES II
Follow instructions to generate sequences

6 Write down the sequence of the first five numbers using this rule.

Start with 2. Multiply by 2 and subtract 1.

| 2 | 3 | 5 | 9 | 17 |

7 Write the sequence of the first five equivalent fractions formed using this rule.

Start with $\frac{2}{5}$. Multiply the numerator and the denominator by 3.

$\frac{2}{5}$ · $\frac{6}{15}$ · $\frac{18}{45}$ · $\frac{54}{135}$ · $\frac{162}{405}$

8 Write down the sequence of five numbers given by this BASIC program.

```
10  FOR NUMBER = 2 TO 6
20  PRINT NUMBER + 3
30  NEXT NUMBER
40  END
```

| 5 | 6 | 7 | 8 | 9 |

9 Write down the sequence of five numbers given by this BASIC program.

```
10  FOR NUMBER = 2 TO 6
20  PRINT NUMBER * NUMBER
30  NEXT NUMBER
40  END
```

| 4 | 9 | 16 | 25 | 36 |

The square root of 36 is 6

10 Write down the sequence of five numbers given by this BASIC program.

```
10  FOR NUMBER = 2 TO 6
20  PRINT NUMBER * NUMBER * NUMBER
30  NEXT NUMBER
40  END
```

| 8 | 27 | 64 | 125 | 216 |

The cube root of 216 is 6

11 Write down the next three equivalent fractions in this sequence.

$\frac{3}{4}$ · $\frac{9}{12}$ · $\frac{27}{36}$ · $\frac{81}{108}$ · $\frac{243}{324}$ · $\frac{729}{972}$

Ma 3/5b — Express a simple function symbolically
SERIES I

1 Write a formula for the cost (c) in pence of 2 kg of apples at x pence per kilogram.

$c = 2x$

2 A girl has £e. She spends £f. Write a formula for the amount (a) in £s she has left.

$a = e - f$

3 Two tapes are x metres and y metres long. Laid together, their total length is 25 metres. Write a formula linking x and y.

$x + y = 25$

4 Chairs are arranged in r rows. The number of chairs in each row is c. There are 36 chairs altogether. Write a formula linking r and c.

$rc = 36$

5 Emma's age is e years. Tariq is three years older than Emma. Write a formula to express Tariq's age (t) in years.

$t = e + 3$

6 A group of d children share c sweets among themselves. How many sweets does each child get?

$\dfrac{c}{d}$

7 I think of a number n, add 3, then multiply the answer by n. The result is p. Write a formula linking these facts.

$p = n(n + 3)$

8 Find the function linking these values of x and y.

x	y
2	6
4	8
6	10
8	12
10	14

$y = x + 4$

9 Write the functions linking the values of x and y.

Input → → Output   Function

a x → ×2 → −5 → y : $y = 2x - 5$

b x → −3 → ×4 → y : $y = 4(x - 3)$

c x → ×5 → +2 → y : $y = \dfrac{5x}{2}$

Ma 3/5b — Express a simple function symbolically
SERIES II

1 Write a formula for the cost (c) in pounds of three computer games at £d each.

$c = 3d$

2 A plank is r cm long. A man cut off s cm. Write a formula for the amount (a) he has left (in centimetres).

$a = r - s$

3 Two fences are t metres and u metres long. Together, their total length is 30 metres. Write a formula linking t and u.

$u + t = 30$

4 Plants are arranged in x rows. The number of plants in each row is y. There are 24 plants altogether. Write a formula linking x and y.

$xy = 24$

5 Tom's age is t years. Mira is four years younger than Tom. Write a formula to express Mira's age (m) in years.

$m = t - 4$

6 A group of p children are divided equally into c classes. How many children are there in each class?

$\dfrac{p}{c}$

7 I think of a number x, subtract 1, then multiply the answer by x. The result is r. Write a formula linking these facts.

$r = x(x - 1)$

8 Find the function linking these values of a and b.

a	b
1	10
3	12
5	14
7	16
9	18

$b = a + 9$

9 Write the functions linking the values of x and y.

Input → → Output   Function

a x → ×1 → ×7 → y : $y = x + 7$

b x → −2 → ×2 → y : $y = 2(x - 2)$

c x → ×7 → +3 → y : $y = \dfrac{7x}{3}$

Ma 3/5b   **Express a simple function symbolically**
SERIES I

10 Write an equation to represent these amounts which balance.

3x grams | 4 grams   y grams | y grams

$3x + 4 = 2y$

11 The perimeter (p) of a rectangle is given by the formula $p = 2(w + l)$.

w

l

   a If w is 3 cm and l is 5 cm then p = 16 cm

   b If p is 24 cm and w is 4 cm then l = 8 cm

12 Write a formula for the perimeter (p) of this shape.

x
y
3y
2x

$p = 2(2x + 3y)$

13   **a** Write a formula for the perimeter (p) of this triangle.

3x
3x
y

$p = 6x + y$

   b What is the perimeter if x is 2 cm and y is 2 cm? 14 cm

14 We can convert temperatures from degrees Fahrenheit (F) to degrees Celsius (C) using this formula:

$F = \frac{9}{5}C + 32$

If the temperature is 22°C, what is it in °F, to the nearest degree? 72 °F

Ma 3/5b   **Express a simple function symbolically**
SERIES II

10 Write an equation to represent these amounts which balance.

2x grams | y grams   5 grams | 2x grams

$3y = 2x + 5$

11 The perimeter (p) of a rectangle is given by the formula $p = 2(t + q)$.

t

q

   a If t is 7 cm and q is 4 cm then p = 22 cm

   b If p is 36 cm and t is 10 cm then q = 8 cm

12 Write a formula for the perimeter (p) of this shape.

x
2y
x
3y
3x

$p = 6x + 10y$

13   **a** Write a formula for the perimeter (p) of this triangle.

3x
y
2x

$p = 5x + y$

   b What is the perimeter if x is 3 cm and y is 8 cm? 23 cm

14 We can convert temperatures from degrees Fahrenheit (F) to degrees Celsius (C) using this formula:

$F = \frac{9}{5}C + 32$

If the temperature is 11°C, what is it in °F, to the nearest degree? 52 °F

Left Worksheet

Ma 4/5a SERIES I

Use accurate measurement and drawing in constructing
3-D models

You need: ruler, protractor, compasses, scissors, sellotape

1 What is the length of this line, in millimetres?

[97] mm

2 Measure each angle to the nearest degree.

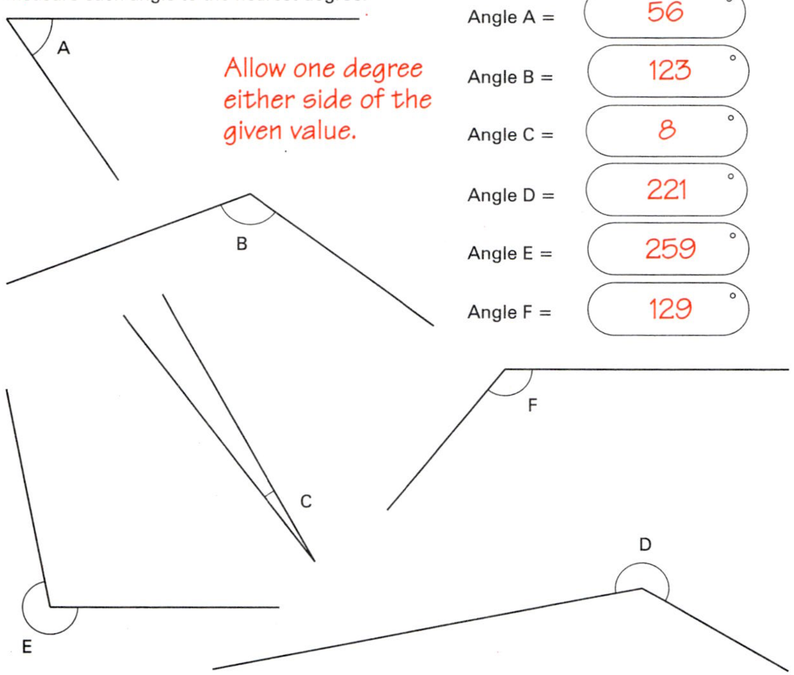

Allow one degree either side of the given value.

Angle A = 56°
Angle B = 123°
Angle C = 8°
Angle D = 221°
Angle E = 259°
Angle F = 129°

3 Measure the sides and angles of this triangle.

a Length AB is 6.7 cm
b Length BC is 3.9 cm
c Length AC is 6.8 cm
d Angle CAB is 34 °
e Angle ABC is 76 °
f Angle BCA is 70 °

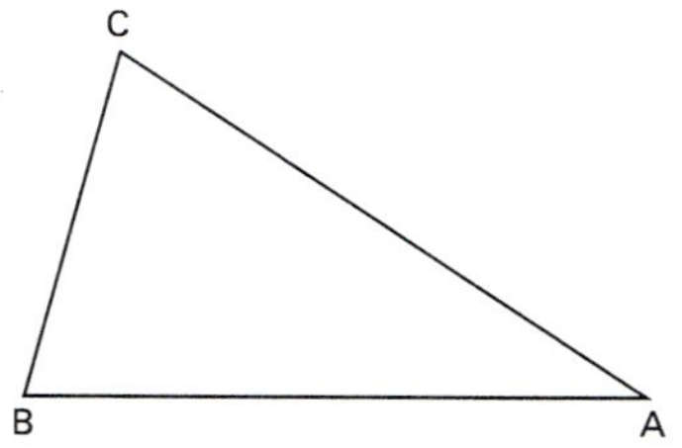

Right Worksheet

Ma 4/5a SERIES II

Use accurate measurement and drawing in constructing
3-D models

You need: ruler, protractor, compasses, scissors, sellotape

1 What is the length of this line, in millimetres?

[76] mm

2 Measure each angle to the nearest degree.

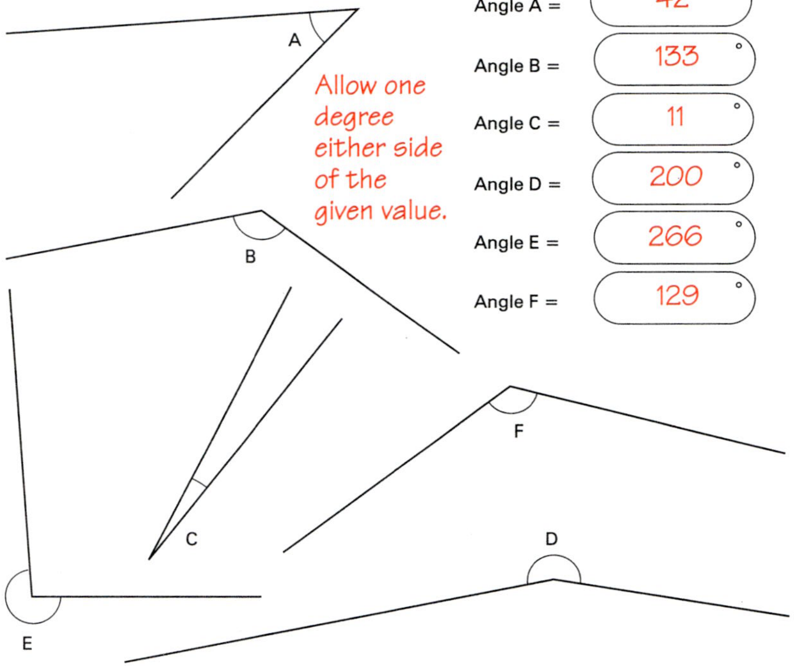

Allow one degree either side of the given value.

Angle A = 42°
Angle B = 133°
Angle C = 11°
Angle D = 200°
Angle E = 266°
Angle F = 129°

3 Measure the sides and angles of this triangle.

a Length AB is 6.5 cm
b Length BC is 7.5 cm
c Length AC is 5.3 cm
d Angle CAB is 75 °
e Angle ABC is 45 °
f Angle BCA is 60 °

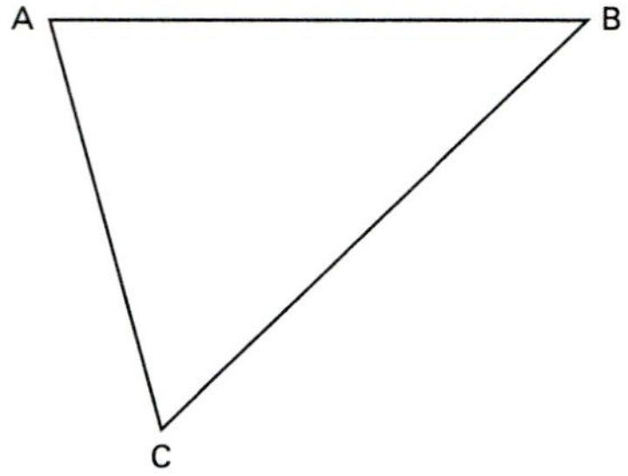

Mathscheck **Name** **Date**

Ma 4/5a SERIES I

Use accurate measurement and drawing in constructing 3-D models

4 In the space, draw these angles.

a A = 37°

b B = 124°

c C = 213°

Mark each angle with the letter, an arc and the number of degrees, e.g.

The three angles should be drawn and marked as shown in the example.

5 Use this space to construct the triangle XYZ in which

XY is 6.3 cm
∠ZXY is 42°
∠XYZ is 47°.

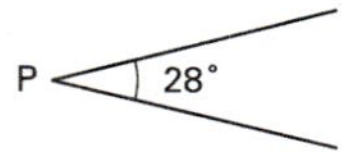

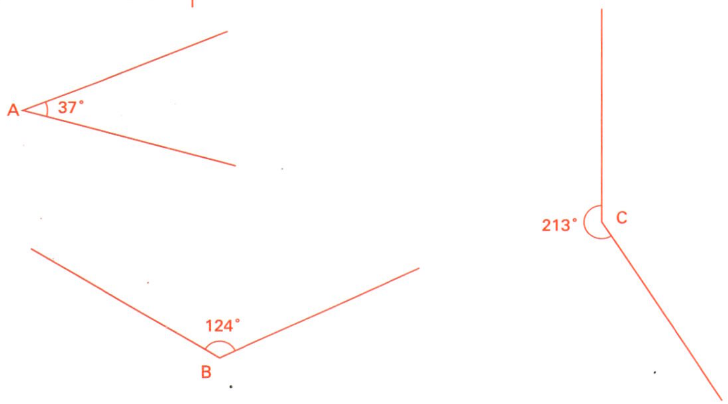

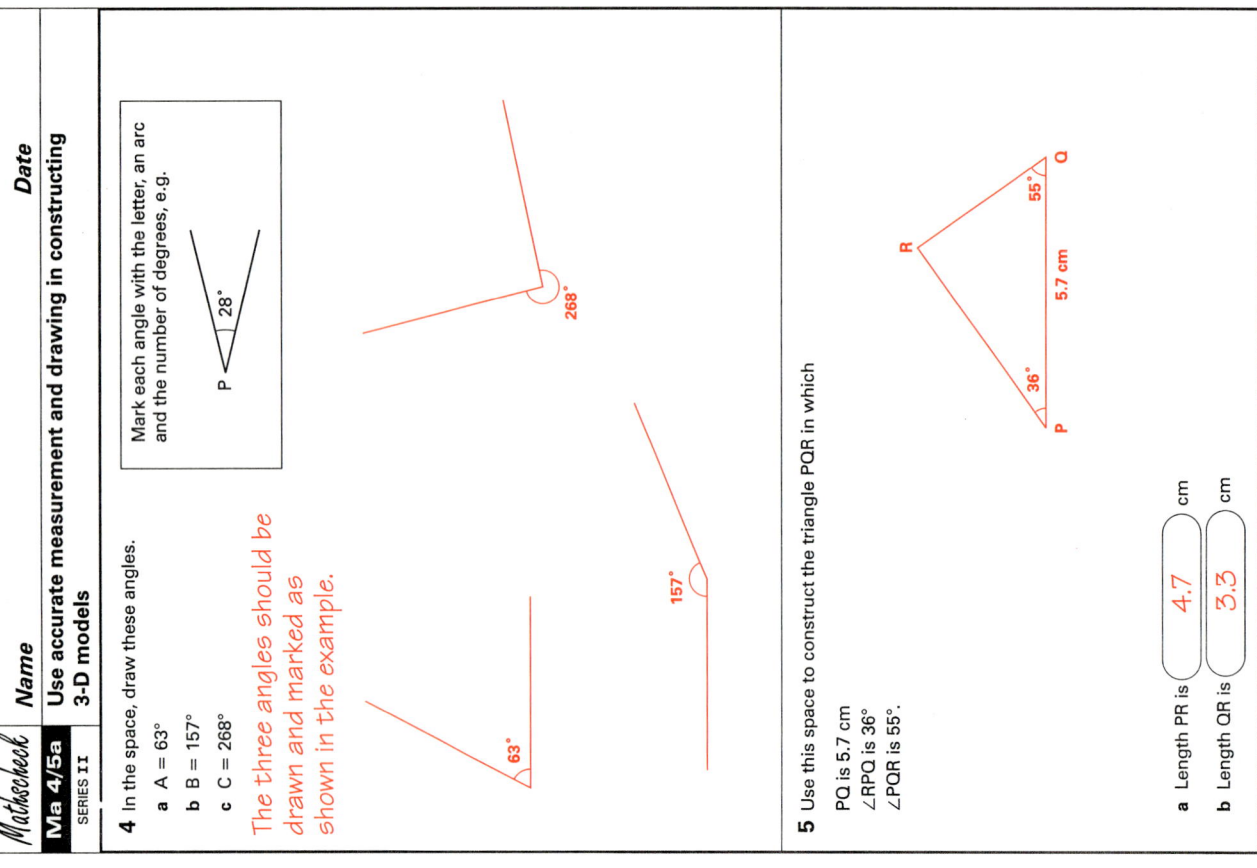

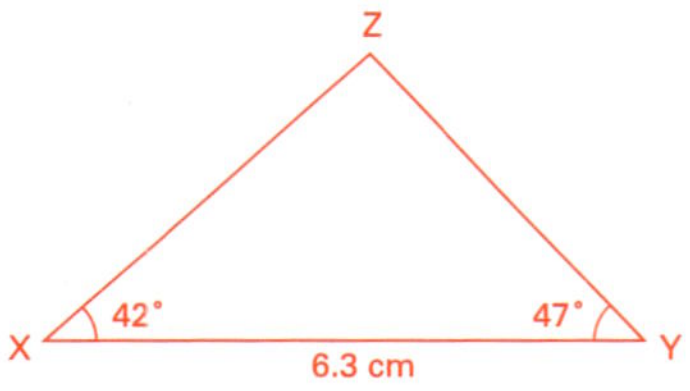

a Length XZ is 4.6 cm

b Length YZ is 4.2 cm

Mathscheck **Name** **Date**

Ma 4/5a SERIES II

Use accurate measurement and drawing in constructing 3-D models

4 In the space, draw these angles.

a A = 63°

b B = 157°

c C = 268°

Mark each angle with the letter, an arc and the number of degrees, e.g.

The three angles should be drawn and marked as shown in the example.

5 Use this space to construct the triangle PQR in which

PQ is 5.7 cm
∠RPQ is 36°
∠PQR is 55°.

a Length PR is 4.7 cm

b Length QR is 3.3 cm

Ma 4/5a SERIES II | Use accurate measurement and drawing in constructing 3-D models

6 Use strong paper or card to construct a square-based pyramid. Use a net like this with the given lengths and angles.

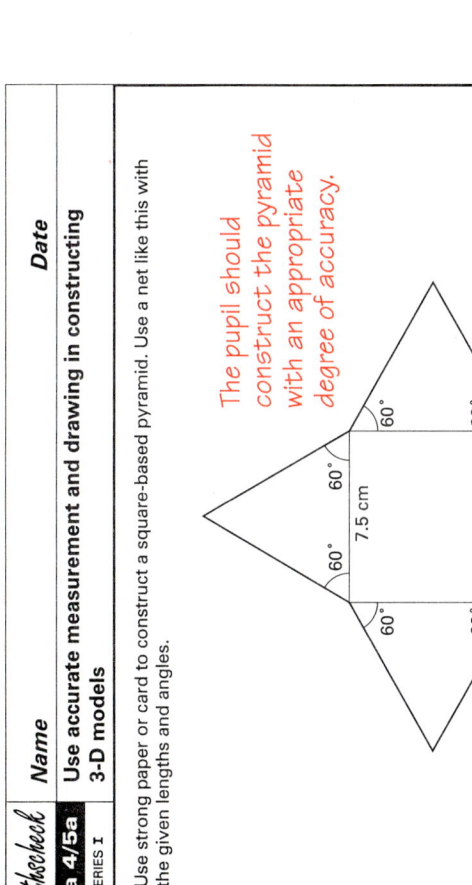

70° 70° 70° 70° 70° 70° 70° 70°

8.5 cm

The pupil should construct the pyramid with an appropriate degree of accuracy.

7 Use strong paper or card to construct a triangular prism like this, with the given lengths and angles.

12 cm

50°

6 cm

The pupil should construct the prism with an appropriate degree of accuracy.

Ma 4/5a SERIES I | Use accurate measurement and drawing in constructing 3-D models

6 Use strong paper or card to construct a square-based pyramid. Use a net like this with the given lengths and angles.

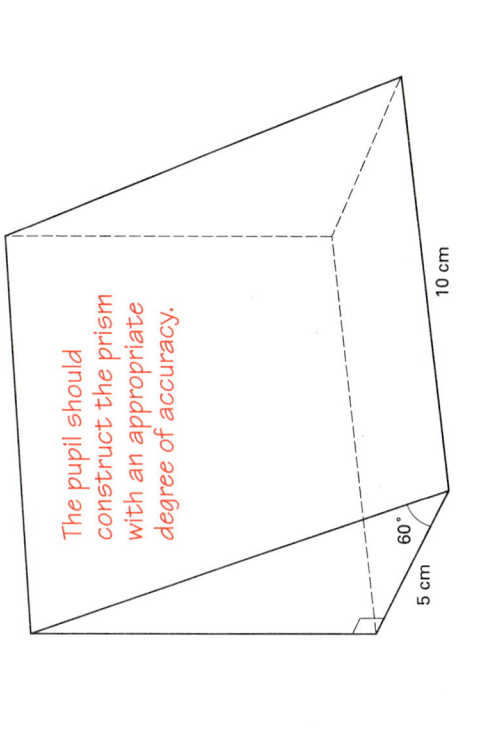

60° 60° 60° 60° 60° 60° 60° 60°

7.5 cm

The pupil should construct the pyramid with an appropriate degree of accuracy.

7 Use strong paper or card to construct a triangular prism like this, with the given lengths and angles.

10 cm

60°

5 cm

The pupil should construct the prism with an appropriate degree of accuracy.

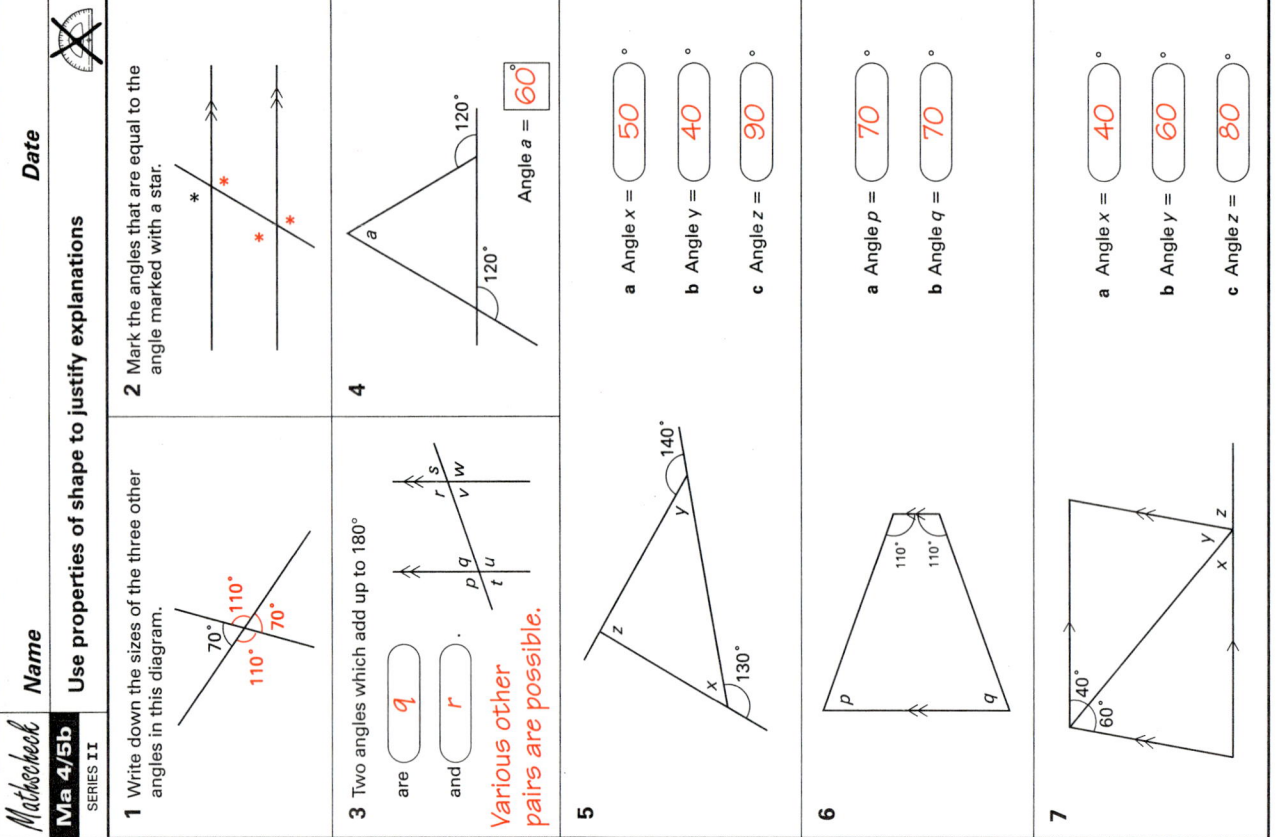

Mathscheck

Ma 4/5b — Use properties of shape to justify explanations

SERIES II

Name _____ **Date** _____

1 Write down the sizes of the three other angles in this diagram.

70° 110° 110° 70°

2 Mark the angles that are equal to the angle marked with a star.

*

3 Two angles which add up to 180°.

are q and r .

Various other pairs are possible.

4

120° 120° a

Angle a = 60°

5

z y 140° x 130°

a Angle x = 50 °
b Angle y = 40 °
c Angle z = 90 °

6

p 110° 110° q

a Angle p = 70 °
b Angle q = 70 °

7

40° 60° x y z

a Angle x = 40 °
b Angle y = 60 °
c Angle z = 80 °

© Collins Educational 1993

Mathscheck

Ma 4/5b — Use properties of shape to justify explanations

SERIES I

Name _____ **Date** _____

1 Write down the sizes of the three other angles in this diagram.

40° 140° 140° 140°

2 Mark the angles that are equal to the angle marked with a star.

*

3 Two angles which add up to 180°.

a b
c d
e f
g h

are a and f .

Various other pairs are possible.

4

110° 110° x

Angle x = 40°

5

120° a b 130° c

a Angle a = 60 °
b Angle b = 50 °
c Angle c = 70 °

6

x 75° y 75°

a Angle x = 105 °
b Angle y = 105 °

7

25° 30° x y z

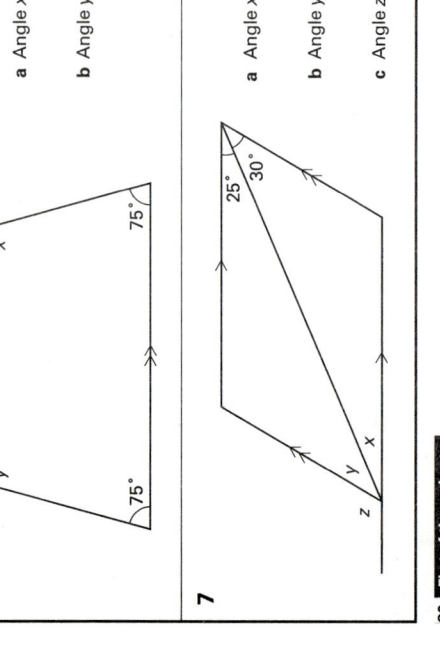

a Angle x = 25 °
b Angle y = 30 °
c Angle z = 125 °

© Collins Educational 1993

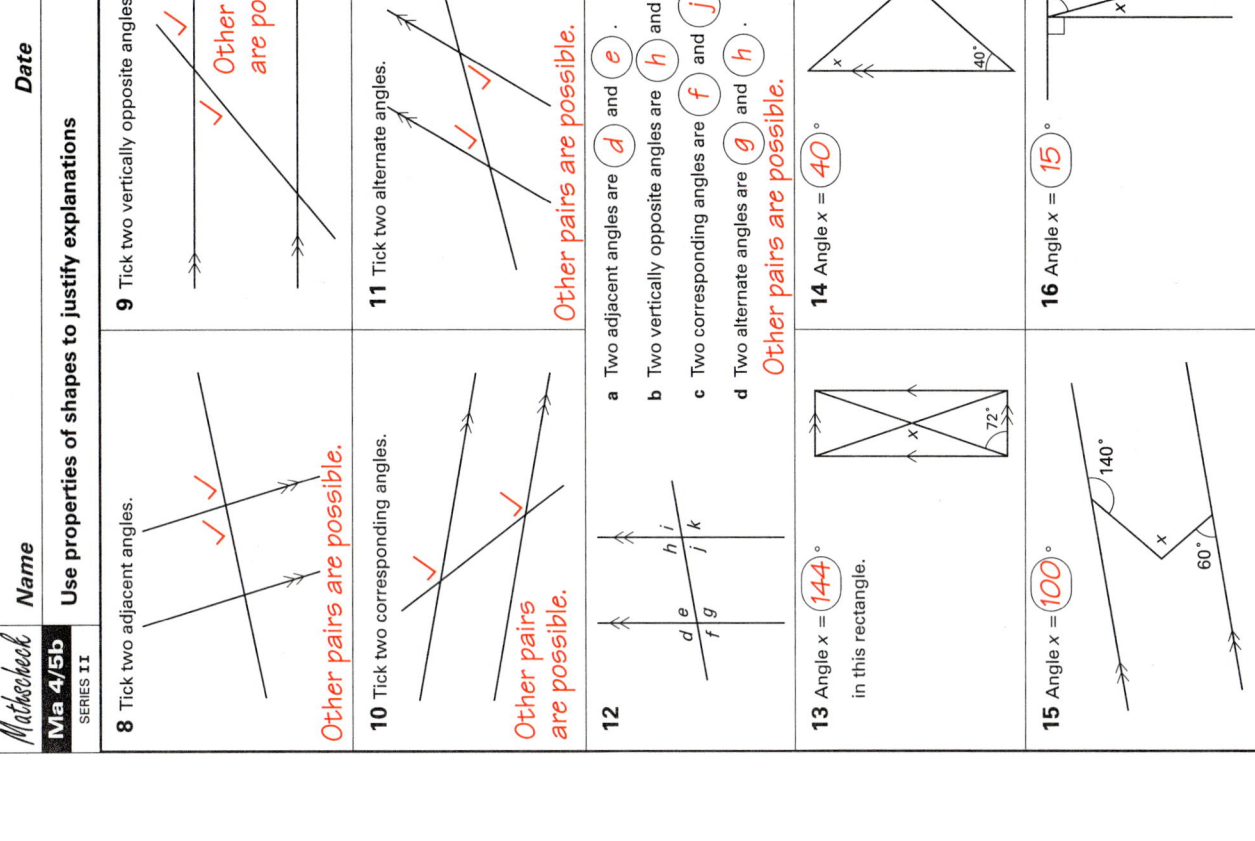

Ma 4/5b
SERIES II

Use properties of shapes to justify explanations

8 Tick two adjacent angles.

Other pairs are possible.

9 Tick two vertically opposite angles.

Other pairs are possible.

10 Tick two corresponding angles.

Other pairs are possible.

11 Tick two alternate angles.

Other pairs are possible.

12
a Two adjacent angles are *d* and *e* .
b Two vertically opposite angles are *h* and *k* .
c Two corresponding angles are *f* and *j* .
d Two alternate angles are *g* and *h* .
Other pairs are possible.

13 Angle x = 144 °
in this rectangle.

14 Angle x = 40 °

15 Angle x = 100 °

16 Angle x = 15 °

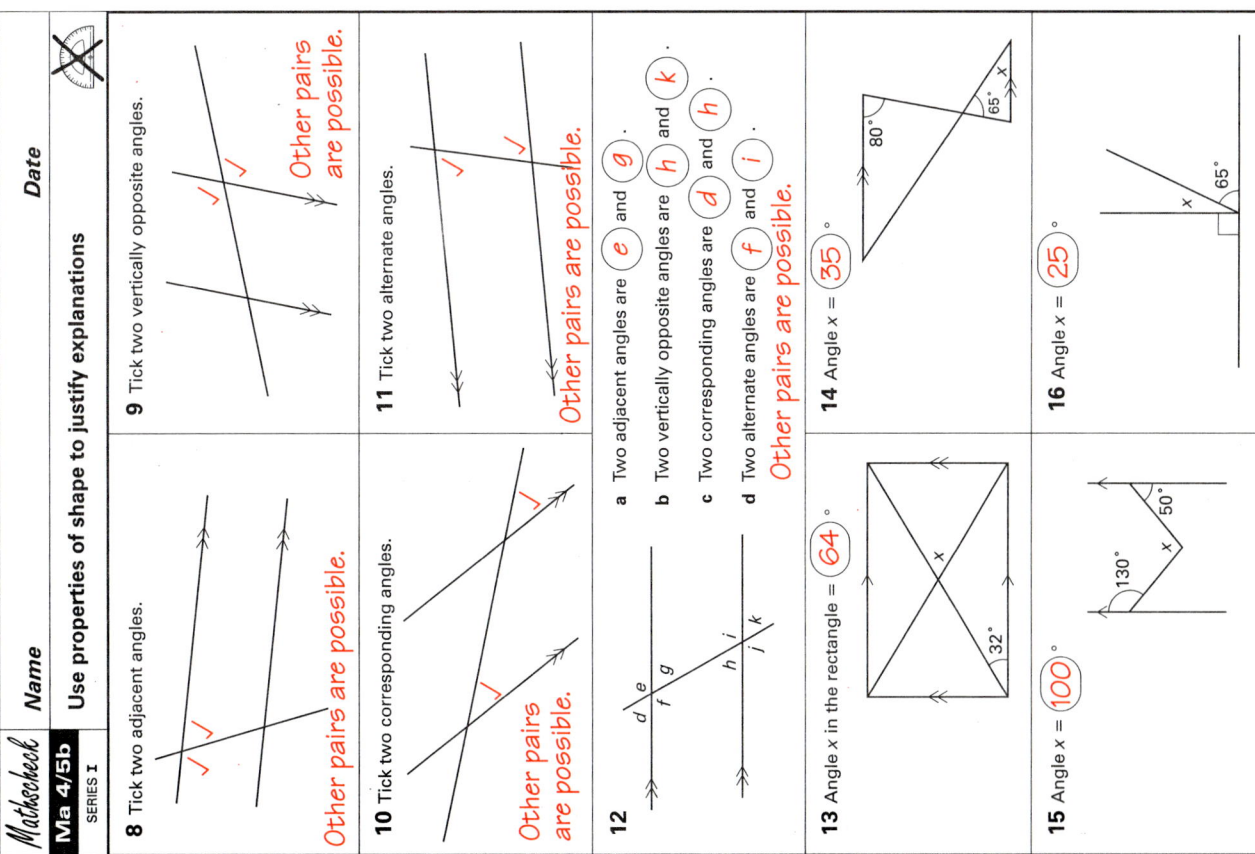

Ma 4/5b
SERIES I

Use properties of shape to justify explanations

8 Tick two adjacent angles.

Other pairs are possible.

9 Tick two vertically opposite angles.

Other pairs are possible.

10 Tick two corresponding angles.

Other pairs are possible.

11 Tick two alternate angles.

Other pairs are possible.

12
a Two adjacent angles are *e* and *g* .
b Two vertically opposite angles are *h* and *k* .
c Two corresponding angles are *d* and *h* .
d Two alternate angles are *f* and *i* .
Other pairs are possible.

13 Angle x in the rectangle = 64 °

14 Angle x = 35 °

15 Angle x = 100 °

16 Angle x = 25 °

Series I

Mathscheck

Ma 4/5b SERIES I

Name **Date**

Use properties of shape to justify explanations

17 A B C D E S H J P

Which of these letters have

a reflective but not rotational symmetry — A B C D E

b rotational but not reflective symmetry — S

c reflective and rotational symmetry — H

d neither reflective nor rotational symmetry? — J P

18 A square has (4) lines of reflective symmetry and rotational symmetry of order (4).

19 A parallelogram has (0) lines of reflective symmetry and rotational symmetry of order (2).

20 Draw a shape with rotational symmetry of order 3. *Various shapes are possible, e.g.*

21 A square-based pyramid has [4] planes of symmetry.

22 This shape has [2] planes of symmetry.

© Collins Educational 1993

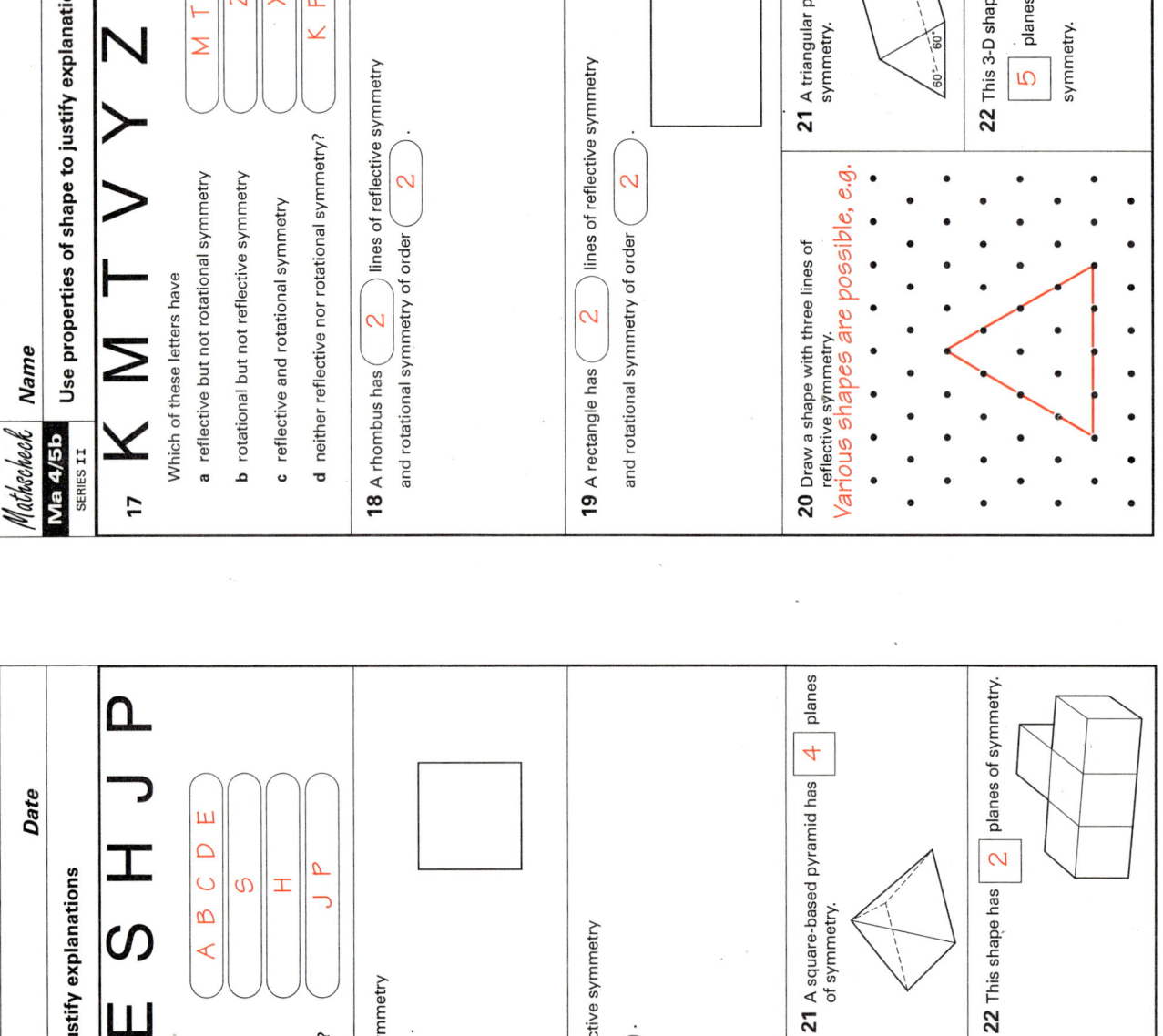

Series II

Mathscheck

Ma 4/5b SERIES II

Name **Date**

Use properties of shape to justify explanations

17 K M T V Y Z X F G

Which of these letters have

a reflective but not rotational symmetry — M T V Y

b rotational but not reflective symmetry — Z

c reflective and rotational symmetry — X

d neither reflective nor rotational symmetry? — K F G

18 A rhombus has (2) lines of reflective symmetry and rotational symmetry of order (2).

19 A rectangle has (2) lines of reflective symmetry and rotational symmetry of order (2).

20 Draw a shape with three lines of reflective symmetry. *Various shapes are possible, e.g.*

21 A triangular prism has [4] planes of symmetry. 60 60

22 This 3-D shape has [5] planes of symmetry.

© Collins Educational 1993

Ma 4/5c — SERIES I
Use networks to solve problems

1 Travelling only across (→) or down (↓), how many different routes are there from A to B?

A
[grid]
B

15 routes

2 This grid is traversable.
Show how on this dotted grid.

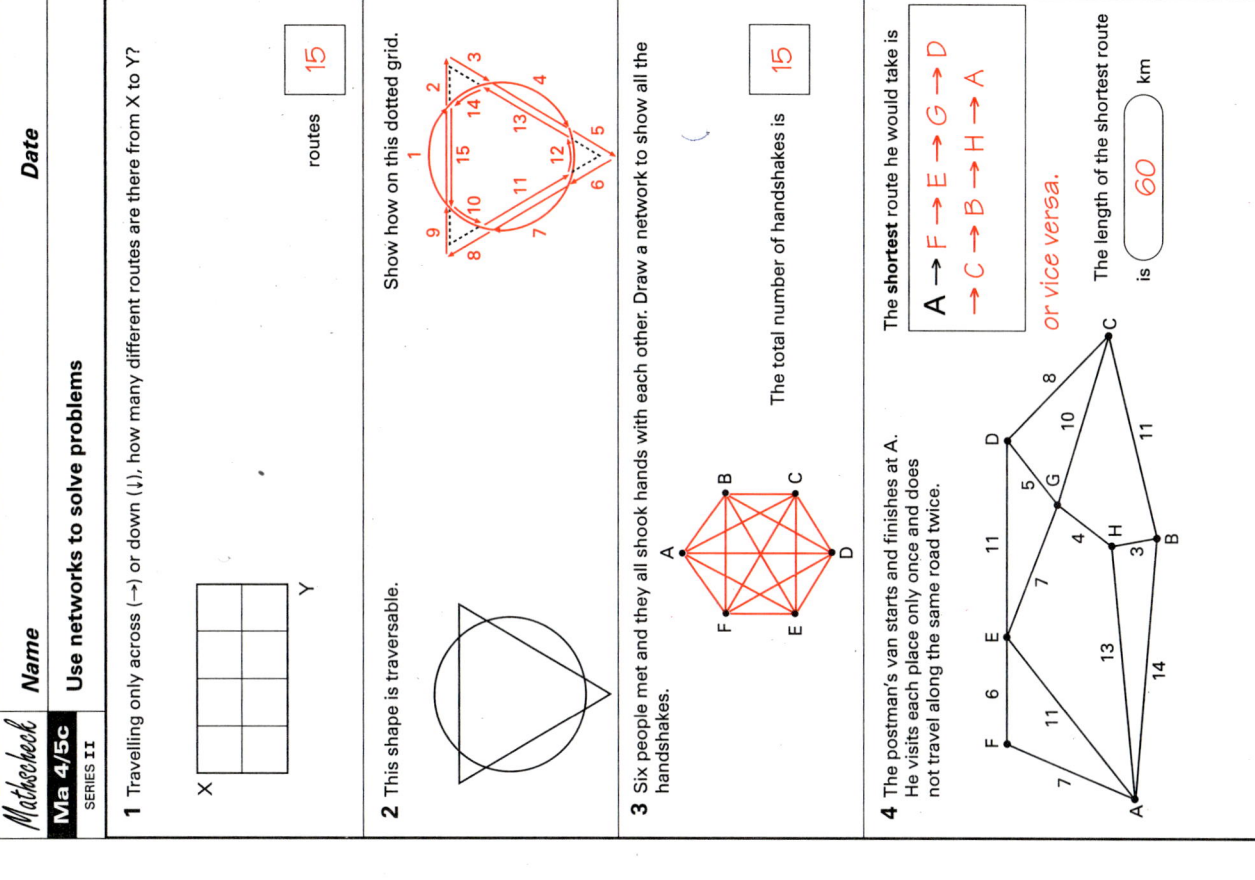

Start ... Finish

Other routes are possible.

3 Five people met and they all shook hands with each other. Draw a network to show all the handshakes.

A B C D E

The total number of handshakes is **10**

4 The postman's van starts and finishes at A. He visits each place only once and does not travel along the same road twice.

The **shortest** route he would take is

A → F → E → G → D
→ C → B → H → A

or vice versa.

The length of the shortest route is **60** km

Ma 4/5c — SERIES II
Use networks to solve problems

1 Travelling only across (→) or down (↓), how many different routes are there from X to Y?

X
[grid]
Y

15 routes

2 This shape is traversable.
Show how on this dotted grid.

3 Six people met and they all shook hands with each other. Draw a network to show all the handshakes.

A B C D E F

The total number of handshakes is **15**

4 The postman's van starts and finishes at A. He visits each place only once and does not travel along the same road twice.

The **shortest** route he would take is

A → F → E → G → D
→ C → B → H → A

or vice versa.

The length of the shortest route is **60** km

Sheet 1 (page 30)

Mathscheck **Name** **Date**

Ma 4/5d — SERIES I

Find areas of plane shapes or volumes of simple solids

1 Area is 9 cm².

2 Area is 21 cm². (7 cm, 3 cm)

3 Area is 15 cm². (5 cm, 6 cm)

4 Area is 8 cm². (4 cm, 4 cm)

5 Area is 36 cm². (6 cm, 4 cm, 2 cm, 2 cm, 4 cm, 4 cm)

6 Area is 36 cm². (5 cm, 7 cm, 6 cm)

7 Area is 16 cm². This shape is symmetrical. (4 cm, 8 cm)

8 Area is 24 cm². (2 cm, 4 cm, 4 cm, 4 cm, 2 cm)

9 Area of frame is 300 cm². (30 cm, 20 cm, 20 cm, 15 cm)

10 Area of frame is 625 cm². (35 cm, 25 cm, 25 cm, 20 cm)

Sheet 2 (page 57)

Mathscheck **Name** **Date**

Ma 4/5d — SERIES II

Find areas of plane shapes or volumes of simple solids

1 Area is 25 cm². (5 cm, 5 cm, 5 cm)

2 Area is 45 cm². (5 cm, 9 cm)

3 Area is 27 cm². (9 cm, 6 cm)

4 Area is 7.5 cm². (5 cm, 3 cm)

5 Area is 28 cm². (2 cm, 4 cm, 4 cm, 4 cm, 6 cm)

6 Area is 27.5 cm². (8 cm, 5 cm, 3 cm)

7 Area is 12 cm². This shape is symmetrical. (3 cm, 8 cm)

8 Area is 60 cm². (10 cm, 5 cm, 2 cm, 2 cm)

9 Area of frame is 275 cm². (25 cm, 15 cm, 10 cm, 10 cm)

10 Area of frame is 480 cm². (30 cm, 20 cm, 16 cm, 15 cm)

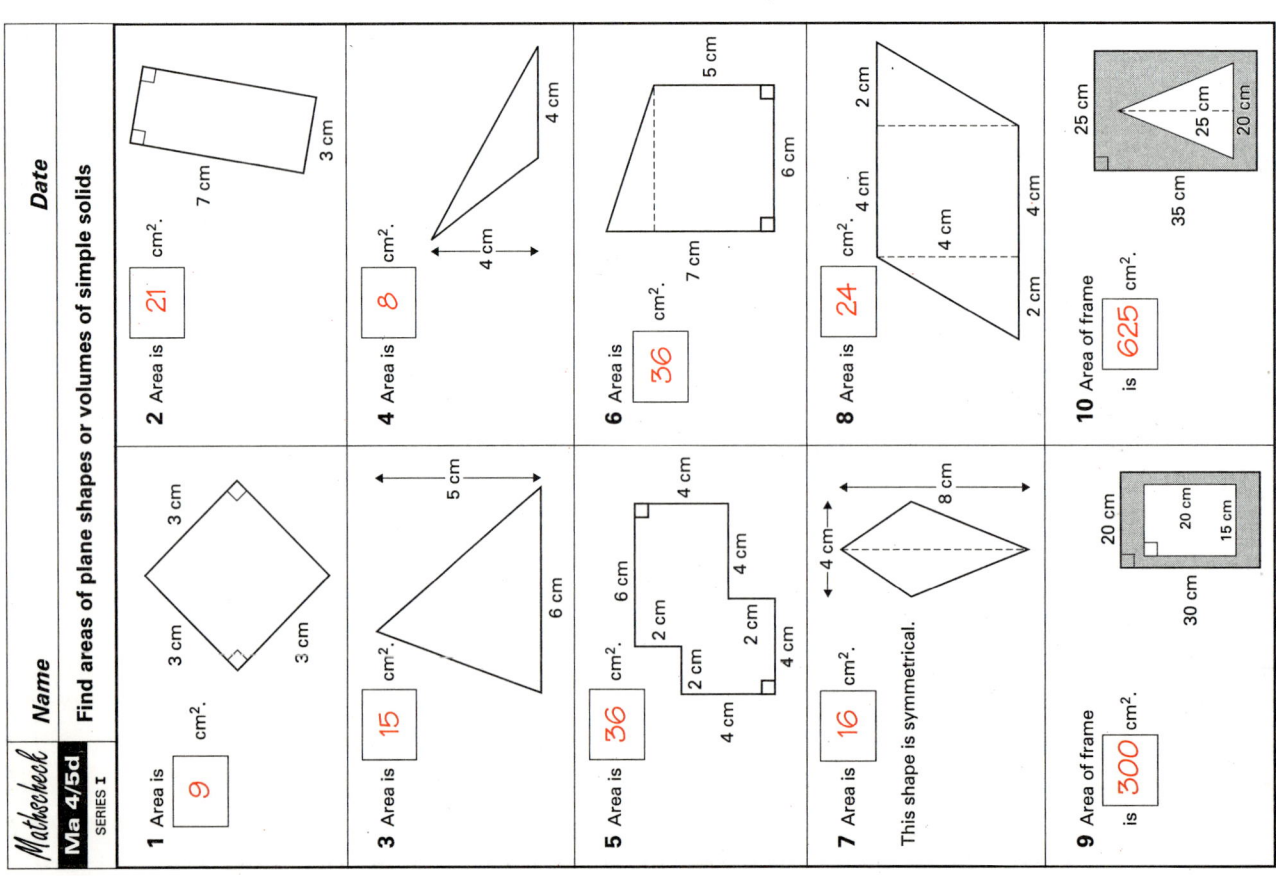

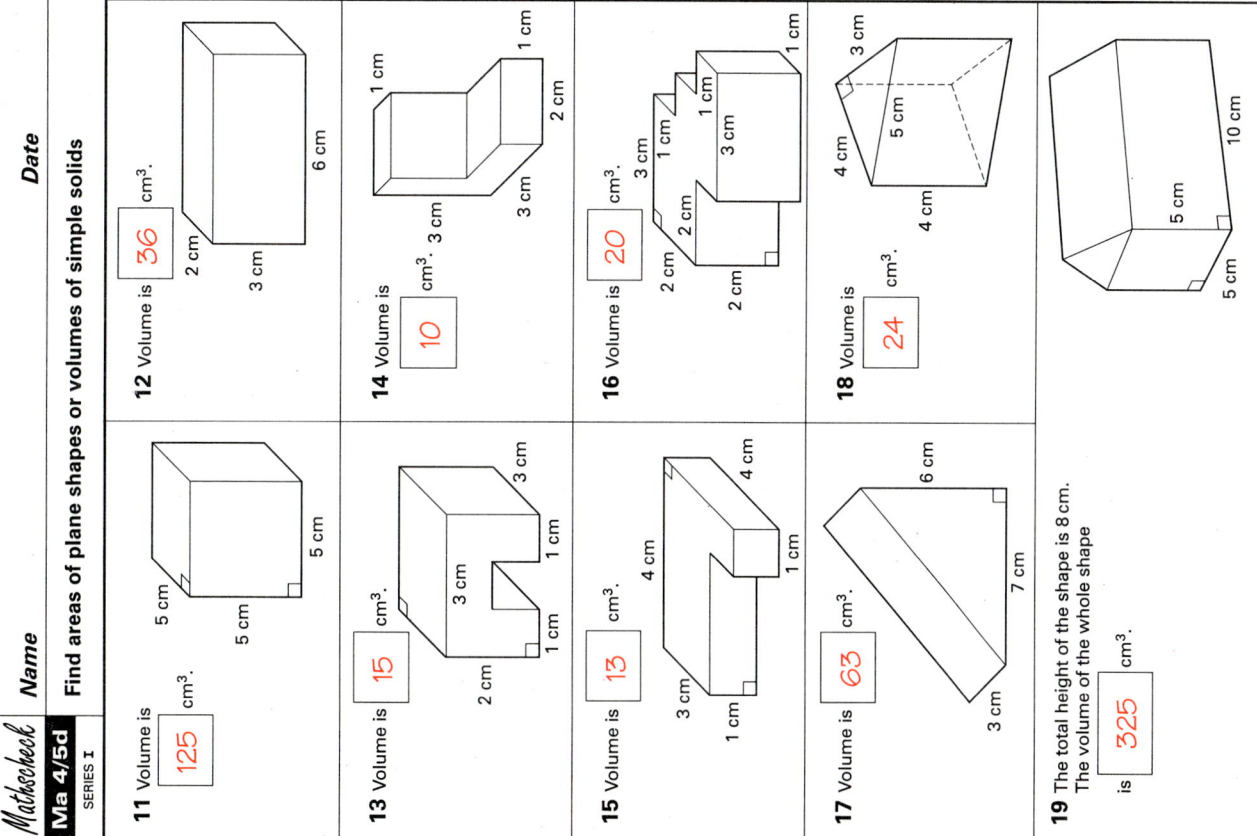

Top worksheet

Mathsheek | **Name** | **Date**

Find areas of plane shapes or volumes of simple solids

11 Volume is 216 cm³.

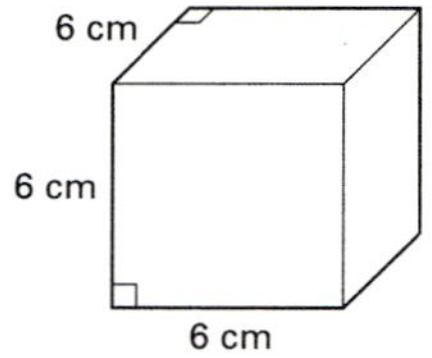

12 Volume is 84 cm³.

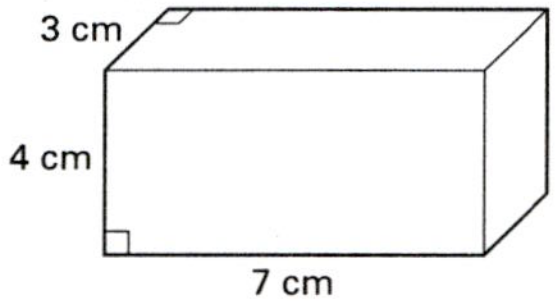

13 Volume is 120 cm³.

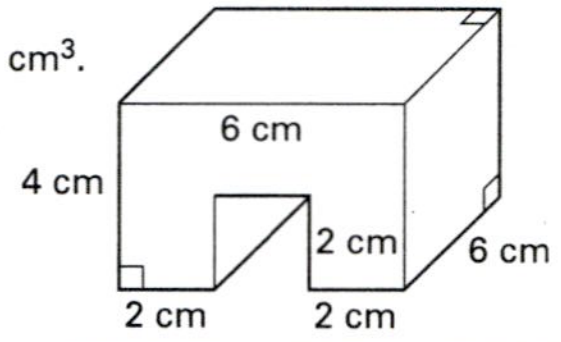

14 Volume is 48 cm³.

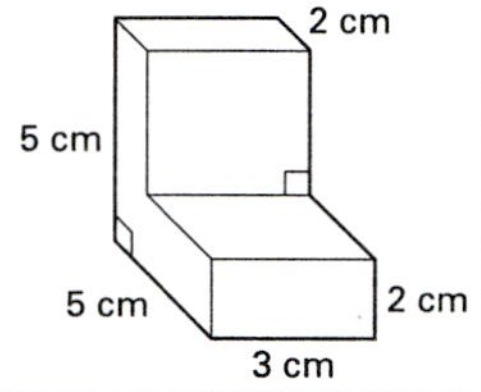

15 Volume is 104 cm³.

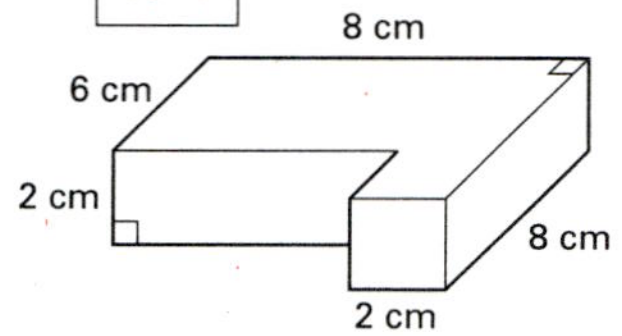

16 Volume is 160 cm³.

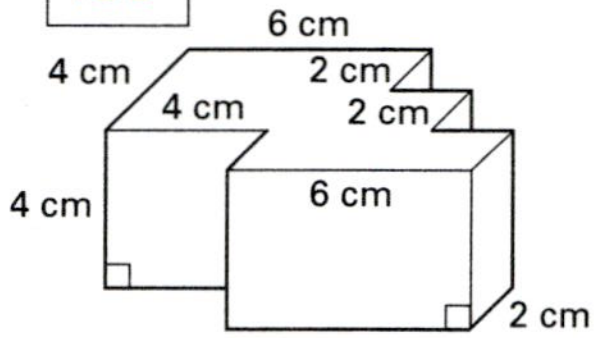

17 Volume is 37.5 cm³.

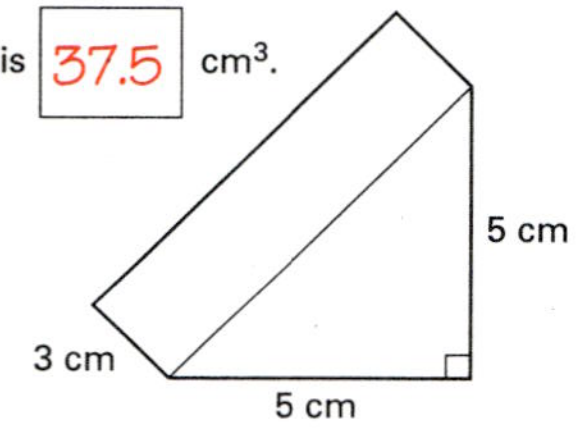

18 Volume is 30 cm³.

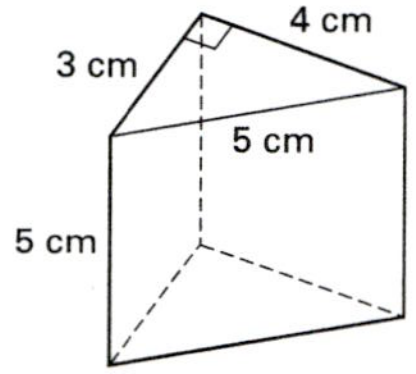

19 The total height of the shape is 11 cm. The volume of the whole shape is 912 cm³.

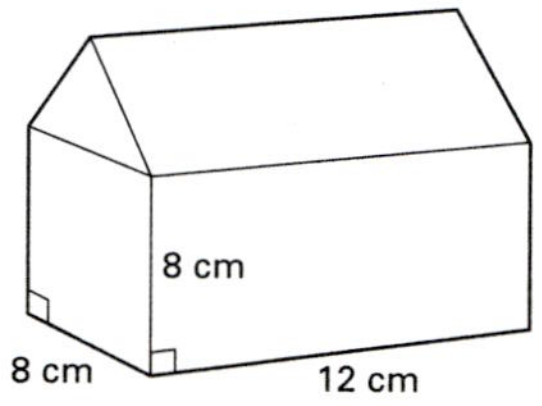

Bottom worksheet

Mathsheek | **Name** | **Date**

Find areas of plane shapes or volumes of simple solids

11 Volume is 125 cm³.

12 Volume is 36 cm³.

13 Volume is 15 cm³.

14 Volume is 10 cm³.

15 Volume is 13 cm³.

16 Volume is 20 cm³.

17 Volume is 63 cm³.

18 Volume is 24 cm³.

19 The total height of the shape is 8 cm. The volume of the whole shape is 325 cm³.

Left worksheet

Name | **Date**

Ma 5/5a
SERIES I

Use a computer database to draw conclusions

Use a computer database package and have your work checked after each activity.

Tick when completed. ◯ ◯

1 Set up a database file to hold 12 records, each containing 4 fields.

2 Enter this data about volcanoes then save the file onto a floppy disc.

Record	Field 1 Name	Field 2 Country	Field 3 Height in metres	Field 4 Condition
1	Fujiyama	Japan	3778	extinct
2	Paricutin	Mexico	2774	dormant
3	Cotopaxi	Ecuador	5978	active
4	Mauna Loa	Hawaii	4168	active
5	Erebus	Antarctica	4023	active
6	Etna	Sicily	3287	active
7	Nyiregongo	Congo	3470	active
8	Demavend	Iran	5366	extinct
9	Kilimanjaro	Tanzania	5889	dormant
10	Popocatapetl	Mexico	5452	active
11				
12				

3 Add this record to the database file and save it again.

Record	11	Wrangell	USA	4269	active

◯ ◯ ◯

4 Sort the records into alphabetic order.

5 Sort the records into height order, tallest first.

6 Name the highest active volcano. [Cotopaxi]

7 Name two active volcanoes higher than 5000 metres.
a Cotopaxi
b Popocatapetl

88

Right worksheet

Name | **Date**

Ma 5/5a
SERIES II

Use a computer database to draw conclusions

Use a computer database package and have your work checked after each activity.

Tick when completed. ◯ ◯

1 Set up a database file to hold 12 records, each containing 4 fields.

2 Enter this data about dinosaurs then save the file onto a floppy disc.

Record	Field 1 Name	Field 2 Food	Field 3 Habitat	Field 4 Length in metres
1	Allosaurus	meat	land	11
2	Triceratops	plant	land, water	11
3	Iguanodon	plant	land	5
4	Polacanthus	plant	land	12
5	Pteranodon	fish	air	8
6	Pterodactylus	insect	air	2
7	Stegosaurus	plant	land	10
8	Diplodocus	plant	land, water	28
9	Plesiosaur	fish	water	12
10	Ichthyosaur	fish	water	12
11				
12				

3 Add this record to the database file and save it again.

Record	11	Fabrosaurus	plant	land	1

◯ ◯ ◯

4 Sort the records into alphabetic order.

5 Sort the records into length order, smallest first.

6 Name the smallest plant-eating dinosaur. [Fabrosaurus]

7 Name the two longest dinosaurs which only live in water.
a Pleisiosaur
b Ichthyosaur

Ma 5/5b
SERIES II

Design and use an observation sheet to collect data

1 A weekend survey of the colours of 50 cars produced this data.

> grey   black   red   red   white   blue   brown   red   grey   green
> green   grey   green   black   brown   brown   blue   red   blue   red
> red   white   blue   brown   green   grey   blue   red   blue   grey
> red   white   red   blue   red   grey   green   blue   red   blue
> brown   green   grey   red   white   red   grey   blue   white   red

a Design and draw a recording sheet for collecting the data.

Various designs are possible, to use a tally count and frequency total column.

b Write down two pieces of information shown by the collected data.

Various answers are possible, e.g. about relative numbers of different colours, or about ordering/ranking the frequencies.

2 Design an observation sheet on which to record data about the number of letters in each word on one page of an encyclopaedia.

a Use it to carry out the collection of data.

Various designs are possible, to use a tally count and frequency totals.

b Write down two pieces of information shown by the data.

Various answers are possible, e.g. relative frequency of numbers of words, or ordering the numerical information, or calculation of the mean and range.

Mathscheck | **Name** | **Date**

Ma 5/5b
SERIES I

Design and use an observation sheet to collect data

1 A weekend survey of the colours of 50 people's socks produced this data.

> black   black   blue   white   green   green   red   grey   grey   grey
> brown   black   black   brown   red   white   green   white   brown   black
> blue   white   white   brown   grey   black   blue   green   black   white
> brown   grey   black   blue   black   blue   blue   green   grey   brown
> brown   black   white   black   green   black   brown   white   black   white

a Design and draw a recording sheet for collecting the data.

Various designs are possible, to use a tally count and frequency total column.

b Write down two pieces of information shown by the collected data.

Various answers are possible, e.g. about relative numbers of different colours, or about ordering/ranking the frequencies.

2 Design an observation sheet on which to record data about the number of words in each sentence on one page of an encyclopaedia.

a Use it to carry out the collection of data.

Various designs are possible, to use a tally count and frequency totals.

b Write down two pieces of information shown by the data.

Various answers are possible, e.g. relative frequency of numbers of words, or ordering the numerical information, or calculation of the mean and range.

Name									Date

Ma 5/5b SERIES I

Design and use an observation sheet to collect data

3 This data shows the results of a 'Welly throwing' competition.
The distances are in metres.

16.2	14.9	15.4	15.6	15.3	15.9	15.8	15.2	15.7
16.0	15.5	15.2	15.7	15.5	15.9	16.0	15.6	15.1
16.0	17.6	15.9	15.2	17.0	15.5	16.3	15.9	14.7
15.6	15.8	14.7	15.4	15.8	15.4	15.8	15.0	14.3
15.1	15.0	15.6	15.4	15.7	15.0	15.8	15.6	17.0

a Draw and complete a frequency table of the results using four equal class intervals.

Various patterns are possible.

Class Intervals	Tally	Frequency
14.0 - 14.9	IIII	4
15.0 - 15.9	⅏⅏⅏⅏⅏⅏III	33
16.0 - 16.9	⅏	5
17.0 - 17.9	III	3

b Draw a graph of the results.

Various graphs are possible.

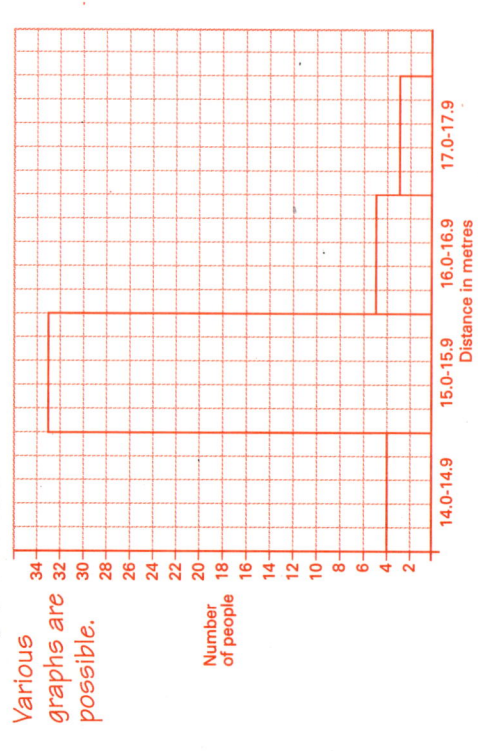

c Write down two pieces of information shown by the graph or frequency table.

Various answers are possible, e.g. relative frequency or mean and range.

Name									Date

Ma 5/5b SERIES II

Design and use an observation sheet to collect data

3 This data shows the results of a 200 metre running event.
The times are in seconds.

30.0	31.2	31.6	30.0	31.4	30.8	31.2	30.0	30.2
29.6	30.0	31.6	30.8	31.6	30.8	29.4	31.6	31.2
29.4	31.8	32.6	31.0	32.0	30.4	31.8	33.2	32.0
30.2	31.2	32.0	31.8	31.0	31.4	30.4	31.0	32.0
31.4	30.4	31.6	31.8	30.6	31.2	30.8	29.8	32.4

a Draw and complete a frequency table of the results using five equal class intervals.

Various patterns are possible.

class intervals	tally	frequency
29.0 to 29.9	IIII	4
30.0 to 30.9	⅏⅏⅏IIII	14
31.0 to 31.9	⅏⅏⅏⅏I	20
32.0 to 32.9	⅏I	6
33.0 to 33.9	I	1

b Draw a graph of the results.

Various graphs are possible.

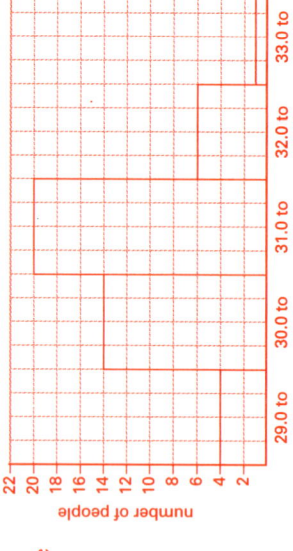

c Write down two pieces of information shown by the graph or frequency table.

Various answers are possible, e.g. relative frequency or mean and range.

Ma 5/5c — Interpret statistical diagrams
SERIES I

1 In a survey, 36 people were asked to taste four drinks and say which they preferred. The results were:

apple juice   9
orange juice   15
lime juice   3
pineapple juice 9

Construct a pie chart from the data.

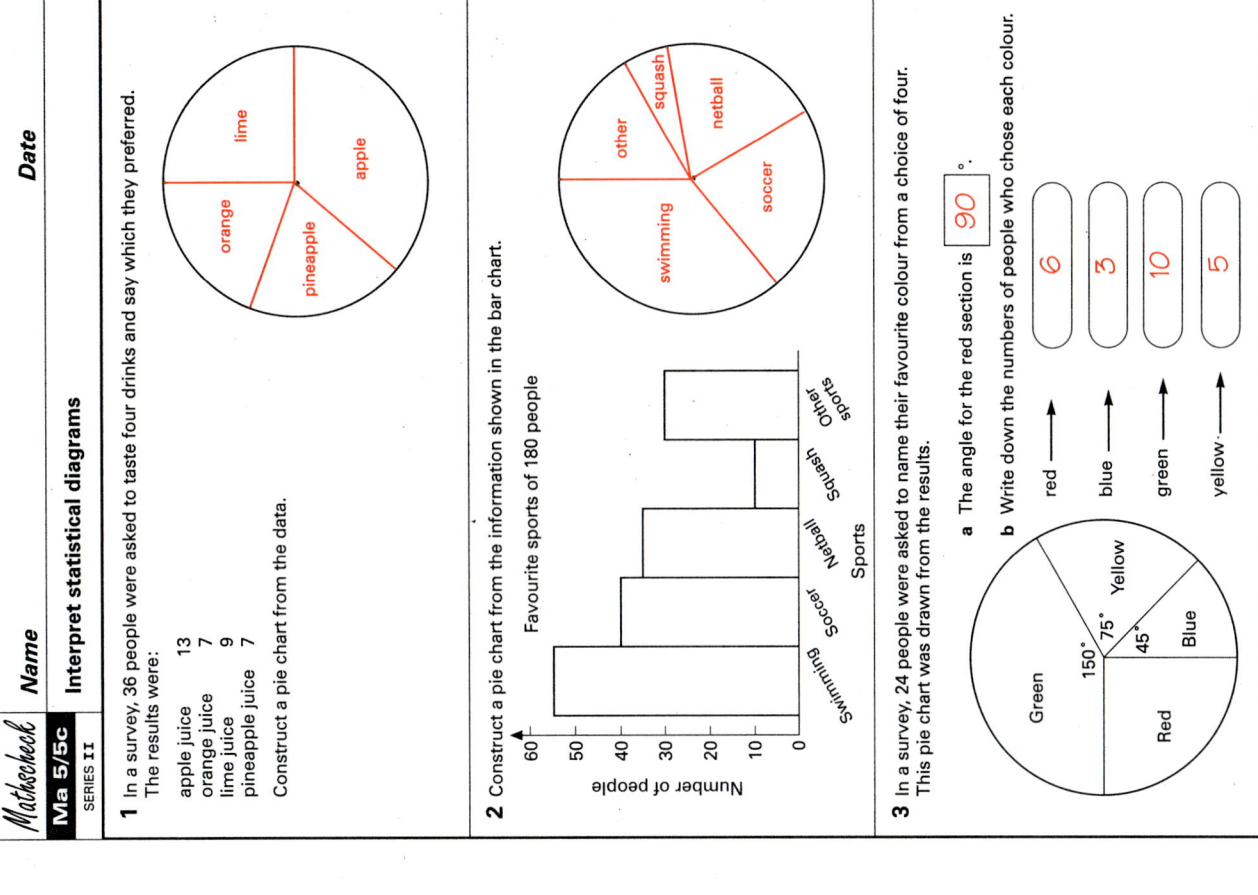

2 Construct a pie chart from the information shown in the bar chart.

Favourite sports of 180 people

Number of people (0, 10, 20, 30, 40, 50, 60)

Sports: Swimming, Soccer, Netball, Squash, Other sports

Pie chart labels: soccer, squash, swimming, netball, other sports

3 In a survey, 24 people were asked to name their favourite colour from a choice of four. This pie chart was drawn from the results.

Pie chart: Red, Yellow, Green (45°, 120°, 135°), Blue

a The angle for the yellow section is [60]°.

b Write down the numbers of people who chose each colour.

red → 9
blue → 8
green → 3
yellow → 4

Ma 5/5c — Interpret statistical diagrams
SERIES II

1 In a survey, 36 people were asked to taste four drinks and say which they preferred. The results were:

apple juice   13
orange juice   7
lime juice   9
pineapple juice 7

Construct a pie chart from the data.

Pie chart labels: lime, apple, orange, pineapple

2 Construct a pie chart from the information shown in the bar chart.

Favourite sports of 180 people

Number of people (0, 10, 20, 30, 40, 50, 60)

Sports: Swimming, Soccer, Netball, Squash, Other sports

Pie chart labels: other, squash, netball, soccer, swimming

3 In a survey, 24 people were asked to name their favourite colour from a choice of four. This pie chart was drawn from the results.

Pie chart: Green (150°), Yellow (75°), Blue (45°), Red

a The angle for the red section is [90]°.

b Write down the numbers of people who chose each colour.

red → 6
blue → 3
green → 10
yellow → 5

Mathscheck

Ma 5/5c SERIES I

Name **Date**

Interpret statistical diagrams

4 This is a graph showing the relation between litres and gallons.

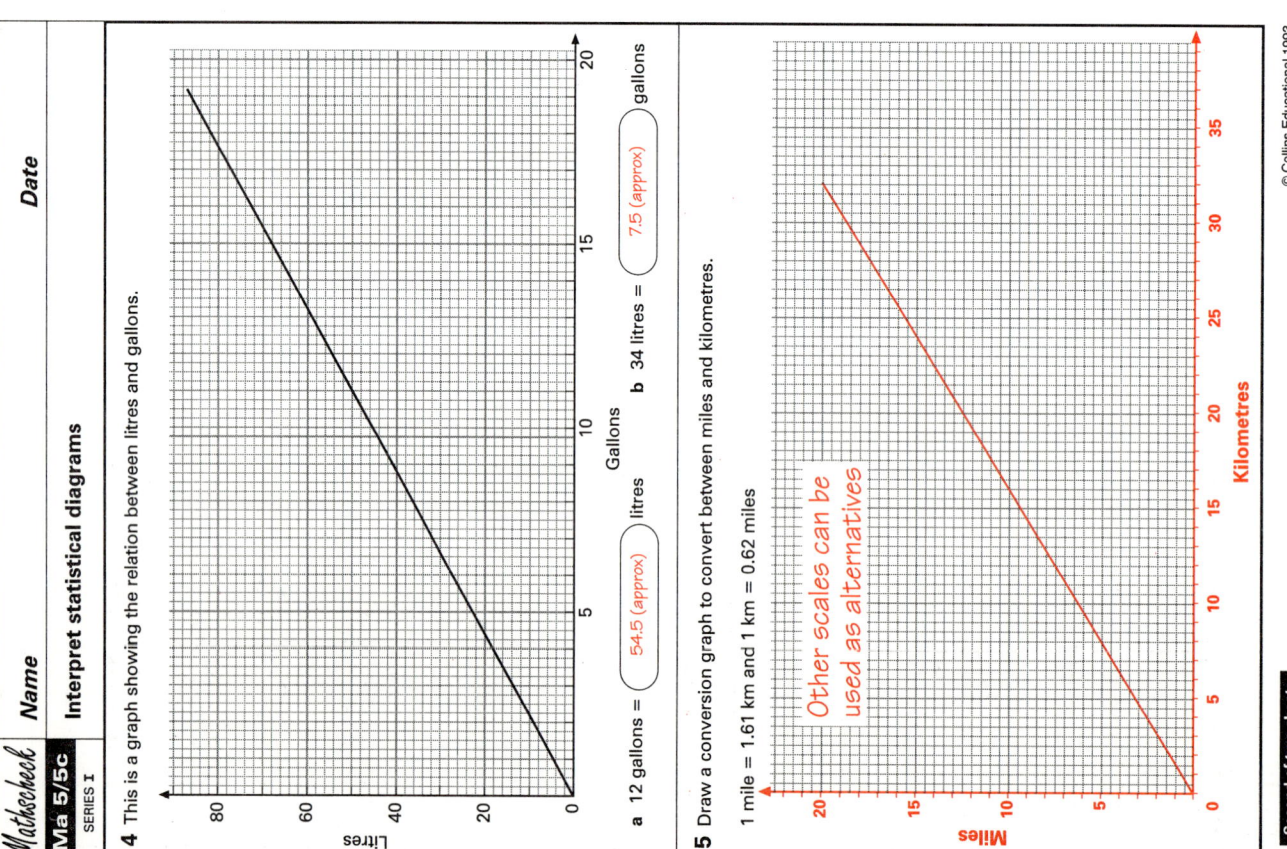

Litres / Gallons

a 12 gallons = (54.5 (approx)) litres   **b** 34 litres = (7.5 (approx)) gallons

5 Draw a conversion graph to convert between miles and kilometres.

1 mile = 1.61 km and 1 km = 0.62 miles

Other scales can be used as alternatives

Miles / Kilometres

Mathscheck

Ma 5/5c SERIES II

Name **Date**

Interpret statistical diagrams

4 This is a graph showing the relation between centimetres and inches.

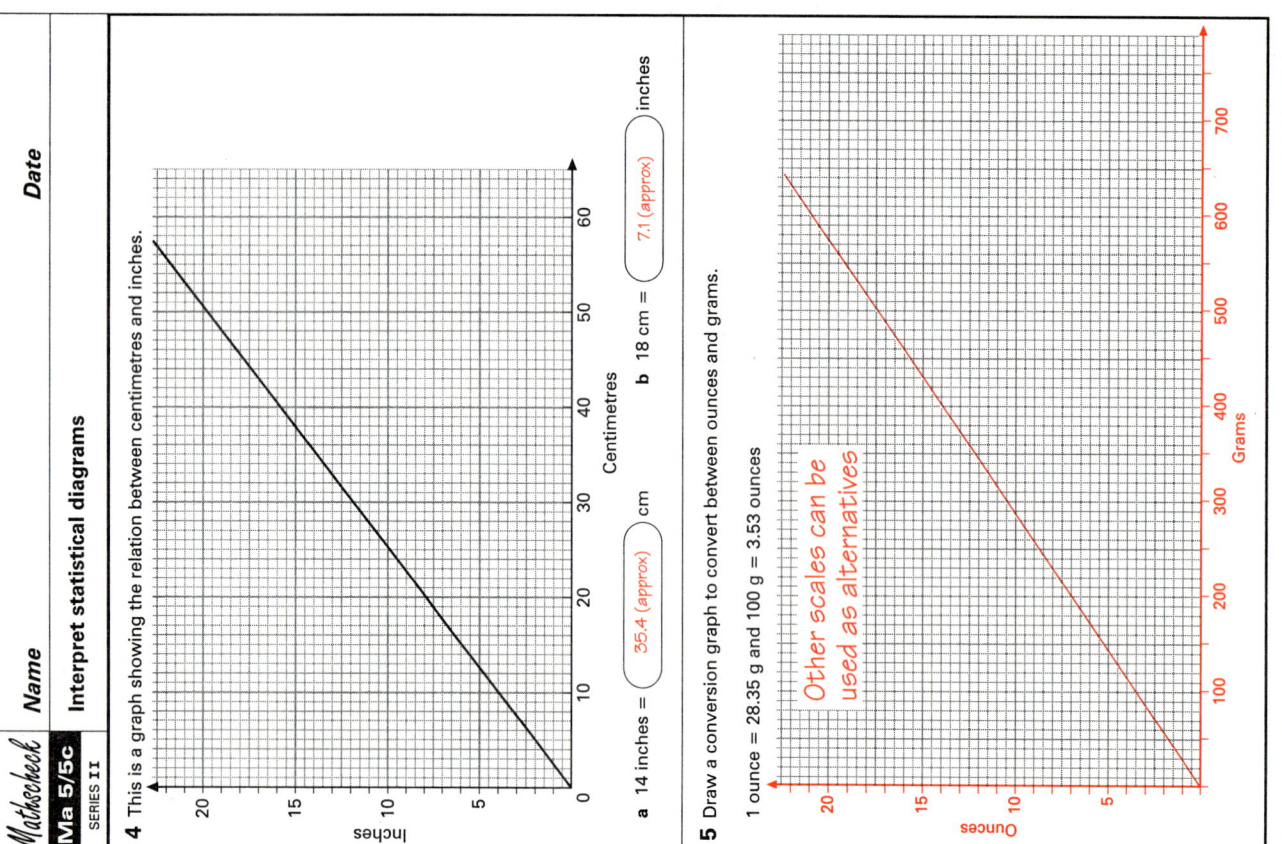

Inches / Centimetres

a 14 inches = (35.4 (approx)) cm   **b** 18 cm = (7.1 (approx)) inches

5 Draw a conversion graph to convert between ounces and grams.

1 ounce = 28.35 g and 100 g = 3.53 ounces

Other scales can be used as alternatives

Ounces / Grams

Ma 5/5d
SERIES I

Use an appropriate method for estimating probabilities

1 Write T for true or F for false in each box.

The spinner is spun 10 times.

RED / BLUE (spinner)

a There will **always** be some reds and some blues.   F

b There will **never** be 10 reds in a row.   F

c There will be **exactly** five reds and five blues.   F

d There will **usually** be at least one red.   T

e There will **usually** be at least one blue.   T

f There **might** be different numbers of reds and blues.

If the experiment is repeated 100 times to give 1000 results:

g There will **usually** be some reds and some blues.   T

h There will **never** be 100 reds in a row.   F

i There will be **exactly** 500 reds and 500 blues.   F

j It is **likely** that there will be **about** 500 reds and 500 blues.   T

2 Which of these situations would allow you to calculate an exact probability and which would have to be estimated?

Write 'exact' or 'estimate' in each box

a The probability that you will throw a 6 on a normal die   exact

b The probability that the next bird to land in your garden will be a crow   estimate

c The probability that it will be sunny tomorrow   estimate

d The probability of picking the seven of diamonds from a full pack of cards   exact

© Collins Educational 1993

Ma 5/5d
SERIES II

Use an appropriate method for estimating probabilities

1 Write T for true or F for false in each box.

The spinner is spun 20 times.

Green / White (spinner)

a There will be **exactly** 10 whites and 10 greens.   F

b There will **never** be 20 greens in a row.   F

c There **might** be different numbers of whites and greens.   T

d There will **usually** be at least one green.   T

e There will **always** be some whites and some greens.   F

f There will **usually** be at least one white.   T

If the experiment is repeated 50 times to give 1000 results:

g There will **exactly** 500 whites and 500 greens.   F

h There will **never** be 100 greens in a row.   F

i There will be **usually** be some whites and some greens.   T

j It is **likely** that there will be **about** 500 whites and 500 greens.   T

2 Which of these situations would allow you to calculate an exact probability and which would have to be estimated?

Write 'exact' or 'estimate' in each box

a The probability that the next car to pass the school gate will be a Ford   estimate

b The probability of picking the three of clubs from a full pack of cards   exact

c The probability that it will snow next Wednesday   estimate

d The probability of throwing an even number on a normal die   exact

© Collins Educational 1993

Sheet 1 (SERIES I)

Mathsheet **Name**   **Date**

Ma 5/5d | **Use an appropriate method for estimating probabilities**
SERIES I

3 You can win, lose or draw in a game of chess. Write down two reasons why the probability of winning might not be $\frac{1}{3}$.

a *Accept appropriate and valid reasons, e.g.*
- *one player may be more proficient than the other*
- *the numbers of ways of winning, drawing and losing a game are not equal.*

b

4 There are four methods for estimating probabilities.

A	B	C	D
Using the idea of equally likely outcomes	By experiment	By survey	Using data collected earlier
Example: [spinner R B G] The probability of the spinner stopping on red is $\frac{1}{3}$.	Example: coloured beads in a bag. Keep drawing out a bead, recording the result and replacing the bead.	Example: collecting and recording data from observation or by questioning people	Example: look at data kept in such places as schools, hospitals, companies or government offices

Choose the best method (A, B, C or D) for estimating the probability that:

a it will rain in London next Monday   D

b if you drop a carton of eggs three will break   B

c a single throw of a die will score 2   A

d the next person you see will be wearing red   C

e the toss of a coin will produce a 'head'.   A

Sheet 2 (SERIES II)

Mathsheet **Name**   **Date**

Ma 5/5d | **Use an appropriate method for estimating probabilities**
SERIES II

3 You can go to school on Monday, Tuesday, Wednesday, Thursday or Friday (5 days). Write down two reasons why the probability of going to school on Monday might not be $\frac{1}{5}$.

a *Accept appropriate and valid reasons, e.g.*
- *the school could be closed*
- *you could be ill.*

b

4 There are four methods for estimating probabilities.

A	B	C	D
Using the idea of equally likely outcomes	By experiment	By survey	Using data collected earlier
Example: [spinner R B G] The probability of the spinner stopping on red is $\frac{1}{3}$.	Example: coloured beads in a bag. Keep drawing out a bead, recording the result and replacing the bead.	Example: collecting and recording data from observation or by questioning people	Example: look at data kept in such places as schools, hospitals, companies or government offices

Choose the best method (A, B, C or D) for estimating the probability that:

a the next car you see will be blue   C

b the tide in London will be high next Monday   D

c a single throw of a die will score an odd number   A

d if you drop ten cups, two will break   B

e the toss of a coin will produce a 'tail'.   A